EXPLORING IRISH HISTORIC MONUMENTS

ANCIENT IRELAND

D1567299

TARQUIN BLAKE, photographer and historian, is author of the bestselling *Abandoned Mansions of Ireland* I and II, and of www.AbandonedIreland.com. He has extensively explored Irish architectural relics and historical sites. His passion is unravelling and documenting a lost heritage. **FIONA REILLY** is Assistant Keeper of Irish Antiquities with the National Museum of Ireland. An archaeologist with wide-ranging experience, she has directed numerous excavations, many of which are published. Her interests lie in medieval church architecture and industrial and historic archaeology.

For Aoibhe and Olwen

EXPLORING IRISH HISTORIC MONUMENTS

ANCIENT IRELAND

TARQUIN BLAKE & FIONA REILLY

The Collins Press

A Faery Song

(*Sung by the people of Faery over Diarmuid and Grania,*
in their bridal sleep under a Cromlech)

WE who are old, old and gay,
O so old!
Thousands of years, thousands of years,
If all were told:

Give to these children, new from the world,
Silence and love;
And the long dew-dropping hours of the night,
And the stars above:

Give to these children, new from the world,
Rest far from men.
Is anything better, anything better?
Tell us it then:

Us who are old, old and gay,
O so old!
Thousands of years, thousands of years,
If all were told.

W. B. YEATS

Contents

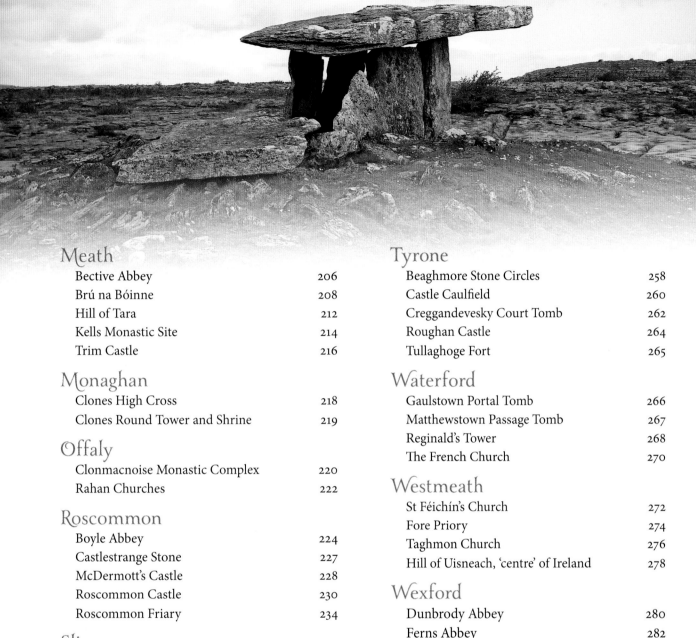

Acknowledgements

Thank you to the National Monuments Service for permission to photograph the sites included in this book. Many thanks to all the OPW staff who helped facilitate the photography, in particular Pauline Kennedy and the guides at the Casino at Marino, Clare Tuffy, Leontia Lenehan and the guides at Brú na Bóinne, and Catherine O'Connor and the guides at Rathfarnham Castle. We are very grateful to those who proof read and commented on the text; Marie Conlin, Margaret Reilly, Alison Reilly, Jamie Lewis and Linda Fibiger. Thanks also to invaluable babysitters – Margaret, Sean, Alison and Marie.

A note on visiting these sites

Although a monument may be in the care or ownership of the State, some are not easily accessible. In the case of megalithic tombs, they often lie hidden in the middle of fields or forest. In the Republic of Ireland particularly, there may not be a public pathway providing easy access. In such cases it is best to ask permission from landowners before crossing their land. Finding a particular tomb occasionally also presents some difficulty: when this is the case, it is best to turn to Ordnance Survey maps or local knowledge.

Disclaimer: Readers should note that this is an information guide and does not act as an invitation to enter any of the properties or sites listed. No responsibility is accepted by the authors or publisher for any loss, injury or inconvenience sustained by anyone as a result of using this book.

Rathgall Hill Fort, County Wicklow:
view along inner rampart wall.

Introduction

National Monuments (Republic of Ireland) and State Care Monuments (Northern Ireland)

In 1871, Sir John Lubbock, a Member of Parliament and a key figure in the establishment of the discipline of archaeology, who had invented the terms Palaeolithic and Neolithic to denote the Old and New Stone Age, received a telegraph from Bryan King, the rector of Avebury, in Wiltshire, England. It told Lubbock of an impending threat to the great prehistoric Avebury stone circle: apparently, a number of cottages were about to be built within the circle, starting the following Monday. The cottagers would part with their interest for a sovereign apiece. Could anything be done?

Lubbock immediately telegraphed the rector and the purchase of the circle by Lubbock was soon agreed. He also bought the nearby Silbury Hill, the largest man-made prehistoric mound in Europe and then introduced a bill to Parliament, which proposed the setting up of a National Monuments Commission, which would protect prehistoric sites against wilful damage. The bill was initially opposed and it was not until 1882 that it was finally passed.

The Ancient Monuments Protection Act 1882, an Act of the Parliament of the United Kingdom of Great Britain and Ireland, listed twenty-nine monuments in England and Wales, eighteen monuments in Ireland and twenty-two in Scotland. The protection procedures and policies of both Northern Ireland and the Republic of Ireland have their roots in this Act and monuments already scheduled under it were included in the National Monuments Act, 1930, which forms the basis of the protection legislation in the Republic of Ireland.

In the Republic of Ireland, a 'National Monument' as defined by the 1930 National Monuments Act is 'a monument or the remains of a monument the preservation of which is a matter of national importance by reason of the historical, architectural, traditional, artistic, or archaeological interest attaching thereto …'. National Monuments can be in the ownership or guardianship of the Minister for Arts, Heritage and the Gaeltacht or the Local Authorities or be in private ownership and care.

In Northern Ireland, State Care Monuments are those historic monuments in the ownership or guardianship of the Department of the Environment. A historic monument is 'any scheduled monument' and 'any other monument the protection of which is in the opinion of the Department of public interest by reason of the archaeological, historical, architectural, traditional or artistic interest attaching to it'.

The first monuments to be taken into State care were some churches and graveyards not in current use after the Irish Church Act of 1869 and included those on the Rock of Cashel in County Tipperary. Until relatively recently there was a tendency to consider only sites of prehistoric, medieval and pre-1700 date as worthy of the title 'National Monument'. In latter times more diverse monument types have been included, such as industrial and historic buildings. According to the latest available lists almost 1,000 individual monuments at 768 locations have been taken into ownership or guardianship as National Monuments in the Republic of Ireland (2012) and there are 1,982 scheduled historic monuments (2012) and 185 State Care monuments (2009), either single monuments, groups of sites or complexes in Northern Ireland.

The 143 monuments or sites included in this book have been chosen not only to represent a broad selection of type and period in each county but also for their photographic beauty. They range in date from the earliest farming communities of the Neolithic to the modern period and in type include megalithic tombs, hillforts, monastic sites, castles, military forts and churches.

A Brief History of 10,000 Years

On a modern map the island of Ireland looks like the last outpost of human occupation before the wild expanses of the North Atlantic Ocean. Its position here, perched on the edge of the continent of Europe, has greatly affected not only its human story but also the floral and faunal colonisation of the island.

Palaeolithic Ireland

There is no evidence of Palaeolithic (Old Stone Age) people living in Ireland, unlike our neighbouring island of Britain where evidence for early human activity has been found dating back to at least half a million years ago. It is, however, possible that the ice sheets covering all or most of the island during periods of glaciation erased all traces of early humans. These episodes of cold and warmer periods, lasting up to *c.* 10,000 years ago, also witnessed the retreat and recolonisation of our native flora and fauna. The latest cold period, known as the Nahanagan Stadial, *c.* 10,000 years ago, saw the extinction of the giant Irish deer, reindeer and red deer. As the climate warmed, plants and animals returned, perhaps crossing temporary land bridges or over a shallow Irish Sea. The ice sheets continued to melt, causing the sea level to rise and isolating Ireland from Britain and Continental Europe. Because of this, there are only about fourteen native mammal species, including wild pig and cat, brown bear, hare and wolf. These were some of the animals which roamed the forests dominated by oak, elm, pine and hazel when the first settlers arrived.

Mesolithic Ireland (8000 BC – 4000 BC)

The earliest evidence for human occupation on the island occurs during the Mesolithic (Middle Stone Age). Only about 400 sites dating to this period have been discovered so far and they generally survive as scatters of stone tools or shell dumps. One of the early sites, Mount Sandel in County Derry, dates to around 8000 BC, and here people lived in circular huts probably for most of the year. These hunters, fishers and gatherers produced stone tools including small, narrow blades called microliths which they set in bone or wood to form arrow-tips or knives. Equipped with these, they hunted food from land and sea, including wild pig, fish and water birds, and collected wild fruits such as hazelnuts, wild pears and crab apples.

Mesolithic people also lived in seasonal camps such as Ferriter's Cove, County Kerry (5000 – 4000 BC), where evidence has been found for the collection of raw materials used to produce stone tools. These comprised axes and broad flakes which were used as scrapers, arrowheads and knives. Fishing, shell collection and fish drying were also carried out here. A surprising discovery was that these Mesolithic people had acquired domesticated cattle and sheep by about 4500 BC (the earliest example of cattle in Ireland). Dugout canoes have been found elsewhere and sophisticated fish traps made from coppiced hazel have also been uncovered, indicating a deliberate management of the environment.

There is very little evidence of how these early inhabitants buried their dead. An excavation at Hermitage, County Limerick, uncovered two rare cremation burials, one of which was probably the remains of an adult male. The cremation had been placed in a pit around the base of a post that may have been a grave marker.

How the hunter-gatherer population made the transition to sedentary agriculturalism is unclear but it seems likely that the Ferriter's Cove people lived at the dawn of what we now term the Neolithic or New Stone Age and the advent of agriculture.

Neolithic Ireland (4000 BC – 2500 BC)

The Neolithic (New Stone Age) is associated with the arrival to Ireland of farming, animal husbandry and cereal cultivation. Cattle and sheep were introduced, along with wheat and barley and a variety of new stone tools, such as flint and chert leaf-shaped arrowheads, hollow-based arrowheads and concave scrapers. Polished stone axes were used and we see pottery being made for the first time. The land was probably still extensively forested but clearance for tillage and pasture opened up the landscape.

Though settlement sites became more permanent there is evidence that seasonal camps were also used, possibly for activities such as salt production, fishing and gathering of raw materials. Large, plank-built, rectangular buildings were constructed in the Early Neolithic. These may have been dwellings or feasting and assembly halls and some seem to have been deliberately dismantled or burnt, such as at Corbally, County Kildare. Circular houses, however, became the most common house shape. Excavated examples include those at Lough Gur, County Limerick and Knowth, County Meath.

The visual impact of Neolithic settlement is in stark contrast to the much more obvious monumental burial sites of the period. The predominant burial evidence is from communal megalithic (*mega* = great, *lithic* = stone) tombs. They have attracted intrigue and folklore over the centuries with many having names such as 'Diarmuid and Gráinne's bed' (p. 196), 'giant's grave' (p. 192) or 'druid's altar' (p. 64).

The majority were constructed in the period 4000–2000 BC and most can be classified, by distinguishing features such as shape, into the categories passage tomb, court tomb, portal tomb and wedge tomb. They usually contain the partial remains of several individuals, either cremated or unburnt. The tombs seem to have been at the centre of a communal ritual where only some members of the group were interred, possibly representing sections of the community. Their construction suggests a high degree of social cohesion, organisation and engineering ability.

The main monument types of this period are as follows:

Passage tombs are defined by their long access passages, which terminate in a chamber, and circular covering mounds. They vary in size and plan and are sometimes located on high ground but the majority are found in low-lying areas. Most are found in the northern and eastern parts of the island. Four major cemeteries of tombs are known: the Boyne Valley (p. 208) and Lough Crew, County Meath and Carrowmore (p. 240) and Carrowkeel

(p. 238), County Sligo. Of the 236 currently known examples about 50 have decorated stones, known as passage art. The most famous one is the spiral and lozenge decorated entrance stone at Newgrange (p. 210).

Court tombs, of which there are over 400 known examples, vary considerably and have a predominantly northern distribution. They are defined by their courtyard area which leads to inner chambers and have been categorised into four major groups: open court tombs (p. 16), full court tombs (p. 242), dual court tombs (p. 44) and transeptal court tombs.

Portal tombs, of which there are about 180 known examples, usually have single rectangular chambers with tall stones (called portal stones) on either side of the entrance. The portal stones often support a massive capstone. Though evidence for their stone cairns is sparse, most were once surrounded by elongated cairns, though oval and round examples exist, and it is not certain whether monuments were completely covered. The cairn at Ballykeel, County Armagh (p. 24) is a rare surviving example and is long and sub-rectangular. Most examples can be found in the northern third of the island and the southeast, with other examples in the Clare/Galway border area and Cork.

Wedge tombs are the most numerous with 540 known examples. They vary in size and most have a wedge-shaped chamber, made from large orthostats (side stones) supporting capstones that decrease in height and width from entrance to back. Some have a small front chamber and others a small rear chamber. The cairn can be round, oval or D-shaped. They are found predominantly in the west with numerous examples in counties Clare, Cork, Kerry and Sligo. A new type of pottery (Beaker pottery) has been found at some of the few excavated tombs suggesting that wedge tombs were first used in the later third millennium or at the transition with the Bronze Age.

Bronze Age Ireland (2500 BC – 500 BC)

The Bronze Age in Ireland saw the introduction of new technology; metalworking in copper, bronze and gold and the development of new pottery, burial practices and monument types. It was originally believed that the migration to Ireland of people known as 'Beaker folk' introduced metalworking and the practice of individual burial, but it is now thought that native communities may have adopted some Beaker artefacts as status symbols without the large-scale migration of a Beaker folk.

Ireland, rich in gold and copper deposits, was an important metal-producing area and one of the early copper mines was at Ross Island, County Kerry. The first objects were made of copper followed by the widespread adoption of bronze around 2000 BC. The gold work is of a very high standard and the earliest was made from thin sheets into lunulae (crescent-shaped neck pieces), basket-type earrings and discs. Later jewellery included gold gorgets and hair rings. Objects made from copper and bronze included awls, axes, daggers, swords and halberds.

Early Bronze Age burial changed from Neolithic communal interment to the burial of individuals in isolated graves as well as in cemeteries and sometimes at Neolithic tombs. The individual could be cremated or inhumed (unburnt) in a variety of grave types such as stone-lined graves and pits. They were often accompanied by richly decorated pottery vessels. As in the Neolithic only some members of the community were buried. As the Bronze Age progressed, cremation without pottery vessels became the only burial method and eventually only tiny, symbolic amounts of bone were buried as tokens.

By the Middle Bronze Age people lived in a variety of settlements including enclosed farmsteads, larger settlements and high-status sites such as Haughey's Fort, County Armagh. Some hillforts have been dated to this period, for example the multifunctional fort at Rathgall, County Wicklow (p. 298) where evidence has been found for settlement, bronze working, burial and metalworking into the Iron Age and later. The most common houses were oval and circular wooden types.

The main monument types of this period are as follows:

Stone circles are found mainly in south Munster and mid Ulster. The Munster group circles are known as recumbent stone circles and can have five free-standing stones (five-stone circles) or a greater number (multiple-stone circles). The entrance is typically between the two largest stones (portal stones) and the stones usually decrease in size from the portal stones to the horizontally placed recumbent stone opposite the entrance. Drombeg, County Cork (p. 64) is an example of a multiple-stone circle. The Ulster circles are quite different, having a greater number of smaller, lower stones. They often occur in groups such as at Beaghmore, County Tyrone (p. 258).

Standing stones are single stones set upright and can be seen dotted around the landscape. Some mark burials, though the function of most is unknown. The large example at Clochafarmore, County Louth (p. 186), is associated with the legend of the death of Cúchulainn.

Stones alignments are a row of three or more upright stones in a straight line. They are associated with stone circles in the north of Ireland.

Burnt mounds or *fulachtaí fia* are the remains of monuments where stones heated in a fire were placed in water, usually in a trough, to produce hot water and steam. They have traditionally been associated with cooking but present understanding regards them as multifunctional, with various possible uses from textile production to brewing and sauna use. These low-profile monuments of burnt stone are found in wet areas and can go undetected until the earth is disturbed. An example was excavated 40m from the stone circle at Drombeg, County Cork (p. 64).

Hill forts are large enclosures with a single or multiple lines of defence, such as Rathgall, County Wicklow (p. 298), built in easily defended areas such as hilltops or in prominent locations. They were thought to date to the Iron Age but excavation of a few to date has shown that some at least were started in the Bronze Age.

Iron Age Ireland (600 BC – AD 400)

Like preceding periods, the Iron Age is recognised by the introduction of new technologies, burial practices and material culture. Precisely how and when this occurred is one of the great mysteries of Irish prehistory. The changes were traditionally explained by the migration of Celtic people from Continental Europe. There is, however, no archaeological evidence of a large-scale influx of people and current theories stress the movement of ideas rather than mass movement of populations. Early Irish literature has influenced our perception of the period with stories of fabled kings, warriors and feasting.

Evidence for settlement sites from this period is rare and where it is found objects are often scarce. Examples include small circular structures identified in counties Cork, Limerick and Tipperary. Only a few hillforts have been dated and some of those excavated, such as Rathgall, County Wicklow, show a Late Bronze Age construction date but continued in use into the Iron Age.

Burial evidence from this period is also scarce, partly because of the continued custom of burying token cremations, the lack of grave goods and because only a minority were formally buried. There was a variety of burial practices, with cremation and inhumation both being carried out. Token cremations, often with objects such as glass beads and bronze fibulae (brooches), were buried in ring-barrows and ring-ditches. The practice of extended inhumation burial (the common method of burial today) is thought to have been influenced by the tradition in Roman Britain from the second century AD.

Distinctive designs in the La Tène style evolved with the use of spirals and stylised animals such as birds. Some beautiful examples survive, such as the gold torc from the Broighter Hoard, found in County Derry in 1896, and on finely decorated bronze scabbard plates. Horse harness pieces and personal ornaments were made of bronze, and gold was still used for torcs and other objects, such as an exceptionally detailed gold model of a boat also found in the Broighter Hoard. Iron ores are widespread throughout Ireland and the earliest iron objects, such as socketed axes, copied the styles or techniques of earlier bronze examples. Pottery vessels were no longer made and were probably replaced by wooden, iron and leather containers.

Some of the best-known monuments of Irish prehistory date to this period. They are what are known as the 'royal' sites of Tara, County Meath (p. 212), Navan Fort, County Armagh (p. 32), Rathcroghan, County Roscommon and Knockaulin, County Kildare. They are steeped in lore, much of which was recorded or (some would argue) invented in the medieval period. Archaeological evidence shows they were important centres of ritual and ceremonial activity for long periods of time.

The main monument types of this period are as follows:

Ring-barrows, ring-ditches and embanked ring-ditches are variations of similar circular funerary monuments. The ring-barrow is a low mound with a surrounding ditch and outer bank. Where there is not a mound the term 'embanked ring-ditch' is used, and where only a ditch is discernible they are called ring-ditches. Some have entrances through the bank and a causeway across the ditch; a few have multiple banks and ditches. They vary in size from 15m to 30m in external diameter.

Hillforts though described in the Bronze Age section, the possibility that some date to the Iron Age cannot be ruled out.

Linear earthwork is a broad term applied to bank, and bank-and-ditch features. It can be applied to parallel pairs of banks, such as the Banqueting Hall at Tara and what are known as the Mucklaghs at Rathcroghan. Some very long examples seem to have demarcated boundaries, the most famous of which is the Black Pig's Dyke, said to have run from Bundoran in County Donegal to Dundalk in County Louth.

La Tène-style carved stones may have been stone versions of timber examples. Five of these stones are known, though the exact original settings for all have been lost. They may have had religious significance. The most famous is the Turoe Stone in County Galway, which might have stood on a summit of a hill. Another, now at Castlestrange, County Roscommon (p. 227), is also a fine example.

Early Medieval Ireland (AD 400 – mid twelfth century)

Unlike preceding periods, where terms associated with technological development such as bronze or iron were used to define the era, the early medieval period, also called the early Christian period, can be identified by the introduction of Christianity. From the late fourth century onwards there was a slow conversion of the island to

Christianity and from the second half of the sixth century monasticism spread rapidly with the foundation of monasteries, such as Clonmacnoise, County Offaly (p. 220). From the tenth century onwards some of the large ecclesiastical sites had streets and numerous buildings that housed monks and lay people (crafts people, estate workers and pilgrims) alike. The monasteries were centres of craftwork and manuscript illumination and owing to pilgrimage and missionary work abroad there was awareness of current ideas and developments outside Ireland. The Book of Kells is the most famous and beautifully decorated manuscript and is on display in Trinity College, Dublin. Burial at monastic sites gained popularity during the seventh century. In the eighth century the Vikings arrived and, though known for pillaging monasteries and causing general mayhem, they contributed much to the island, founding towns such as Dublin and Limerick and introducing coinage. Their graves can be identified because they were buried with distinctive, personal items such as oval brooches and weapons. The final century in this period was one of great change with reform of the Church and the introduction of new styles such as Romanesque. The layout of monastic sites also changed completely with the introduction of new monastic orders such as the Cistercians.

Settlement was mostly rural with the exception of the Viking trading centres and some of the large ecclesiastical sites. The most common and obvious settlement type is the ringfort and there are more than 45,000 known to exist in Ireland today. These were farmsteads and are usually located near fertile land. Houses were round or rectangular/square in plan and there is evidence to suggest that the rectangular house plan replaced the circular; Rathmullan, County Down is an example. Other settlements included crannogs, which are artificial islands or natural islands. They were the homes of the wealthy and some, such as Lagore, County Meath, were royal sites.

Metalworking reached its pinnacle in the eighth century, under the patronage of powerful dynasties, with the production of exquisite objects such as the Tara Brooch, Derrynaflan paten and the Ardagh Chalice, all of which are on display in the National Museum, Dublin. Patterns and styles used in metalworking were also influential in the decoration of both perishable objects such as wood and illuminated manuscripts and stone sculpture for example the high crosses at Ahenny, County Tipperary (p. 248).

The main monument types of this period are as follows:

Ecclesiastical enclosed sites such as Clonmacnoise, Armagh and Kells were large monasteries enclosed with banks, ditches and walls and even to this day their layout can often be seen in the street plan of a town, such as Kells, County Meath (p. 214). Monastic buildings included several churches, guest houses, round towers, communal buildings, workshops and sleeping quarters with the sacred buildings often separated from the secular aspects of the monastery. High crosses and cross slabs were also a feature of these monastic sites. Small ecclesiastical sites such as Reask, County Kerry and hermitages such as Skellig Michael, County Kerry (p. 134) also existed.

Churches from this period were first built of timber. Though none survives, evidence for them has been found in archaeological excavation (Church Island, County Kerry), as depictions in illuminated manuscripts (for example, the depiction of the Temple in Jerusalem in the Book of Kells), as literary references and finally through features on churches such as *antae*. These are where the side walls of a stone church protrude past the gables, and have no practical function in a stone church, such as at Kilmalkedar Church, County Kerry (p. 128). Early stone churches are difficult to date because of their lack of decorative features. The earliest reference to a stone church is to Duleek, County Meath, in the Annals of Ulster in 724 and it is not until the eleventh and twelfth centuries that references become more frequent. The dating of sites such as the corbelled Gallarus Oratory in County Kerry (p. 127) has been controversial, with dates from the seventh to ninth centuries and the twelfth century being suggested. In the twelfth century we see the development of the Romanesque style and the use of nave-and-chancel churches. It is thought that Romanesque was first introduced to Ireland with the construction of Cormac's Chapel on the Rock of Cashel, County Tipperary (p. 256) which was consecrated in 1134. This style was adopted by masons to Irish tastes and Hiberno-Romanesque style can be seen mostly on doorways, windows and chancel arches. Examples are Kilmalkedar, County Kerry (p. 128), Clonfert Cathedral, County Galway and Rahan churches, County Offaly (p. 222).

Round towers were usually built to the northwest or southwest of a church, with their doors facing the church. Many survive to a height of 20m or more, though few possess their conical caps. They are between three and eight storeys high, with a door set above ground level. Several possible dates have been suggested but it is likely that they date to the twelfth century and some such as Timahoe, County Laois (p. 162) have Romanesque features. Their name in Irish, *cloicthech,* betrays their principal function as bell towers, though they were also used to house relics and were places of refuge.

High crosses are free-standing stone crosses which were developed in the eighth to the tenth centuries, with a revival in the late eleventh and twelfth centuries. They were erected at monastic sites, at the boundaries of sacred areas, especially at gateways and in the courtyard to the west of the principal church. As well as demarcating holy areas they were used as objects of devotion and reflection. They can be divided chronologically into four groups based on their decoration. The decoration of the first type was based on metal-covered wooden crosses, for example the crosses at Ahenny, County Tipperary (p. 248) where the stone bosses resemble the glass studs used in metalwork. Human figures are confined to the base while the main section of the cross is carved with insular patterns. The second group is decorated with insular patterns and scriptural iconography and developed during the first half of the ninth century, such as the South Cross, Kells, County Meath (p. 214). In the third group, which developed by the beginning of the tenth century, scriptural scenes and figural iconography predominated; the South Cross (Cross of Muiredach), Monasterboice, County Louth (p. 190) is an example. The fourth group belongs to the Church reform period of the late eleventh and twelfth centuries. These crosses did not always have the distinctive ring surrounding the head of the earlier crosses. The cross at Dysert O' Dea, County Clare (p. 52) is a good example of this type.

Ogham stones were carved with inscriptions in the ogham alphabet. This alphabet, of twenty basic letters, is thought to have been based on the Latin alphabet and is the earliest form of written Irish originating in the fourth century. The letters were inscribed along the edge of the stone and were formed by parallel lines. Most examples were commemorative, for example a holed example at Kilmalkedar Church, which reads 'Mael Inbir son of Brocán' (p. 129). There is some debate as to whether they are Christian or pagan monuments with examples existing from both traditions.

Ringforts are earthen or stone-built enclosures and were the farmsteads of the early medieval period. They are known as univallate when they have a single enclosing element and multivallate when they are surrounded by more than one ring. The size of the enclosed area and the number of banks or walls are an indication of status and wealth. Though the most numerous field monuments, few have been protected as National Monuments. The few that have are usually stone structures such as Leacanabuile, County Kerry.

Crannogs are dwelling places built on artificial islands or islands in lakes. They are usually high-status sites such as Lagore, County Meath, which was a royal site and the seat of the kings of Southern Brega.

Souterrains are underground chambers and are usually associated with ringforts. They were constructed of drystone walling or were wood lined and can be simple, straight passages or complicated, winding passages with chambers. They are thought to have been used for storage and refuge. An example dug into an earlier monument can be seen at Dowth passage tomb, County Meath (p. 209).

Promontory forts are thought to have their origins in the Iron or Bronze Ages and some continued in use up to as late as the seventeenth century, for example Dooneendermotmore, County Cork. They were located at coastal sites on land jutting out into the sea or inland on areas of high ground. It was easy to ward off attack by building defences across the neck of the promontory. Located in inhospitable areas, some may have been temporary refuges.

Late Medieval Ireland (mid twelfth century – mid sixteenth century)

In the years prior to the arrival of the Anglo-Normans there was a power struggle raging between Murtough MacLoughlainn of Aileach, the most powerful king in Ireland, and Rory O'Connor, King of Connacht. By 1166, Dermot MacMurrough of Leinster, who had supported the now dead MacLoughlainn, was under pressure from his enemies. This led to him making an alliance with Henry II of England and inviting Strongbow and his followers to Ireland to restore him to power. It is because of this personal conflict that the Anglo-Normans initially arrived in Wexford in 1169, with Strongbow following in 1170 and Henry II himself in 1171. They had an enormous impact on Irish society, which resulted in a changed landscape, the introduction of new patterns of settlement, farming practices, language, warfare and architectural styles. Our legal system, law courts and representative parliament all find roots in this period and even the first Irish parliament, called by Edward I in 1297, was during this time.

At first the Anglo-Normans built earth-and-timber castles for defence and sometimes, as the colony became established, replaced them with stone castles. In the preceding period, settlement was mostly rural in scattered ringforts with few urban areas but now existing towns and villages grew and many more were constructed. Towns often had defensive walls. Rural settlement within the colony was arranged in manors held by lords, with tenants of varying grades paying rent or doing military service. The land was farmed in rotation, in large open fields with individuals working strips scattered throughout the field. This system proved very productive and in the late thirteenth century food was being exported for the Crown's overseas armies. Wool production was also an important part of the economy and was both exported and sold on the home market. Gothic architecture was introduced at the end of the twelfth century by the Anglo-Normans, with the best early Gothic examples being built in the early thirteenth century. The Cistercian abbeys of Inch (p. 98) and Grey (p. 96) in County Down are considered the earliest examples of this style, which is recognised by the use of tall, graceful lancet windows and pointed arches. Found predominantly west of the Shannon, in the kingdoms of Connacht and Thomond, a style developed known as the 'School of the West', where Romanesque and Gothic styles entwined. Parts of the Cistercian abbey at Boyle, County Roscommon (p. 224) and Corcomroe Abbey, County Clare (p. 50) are examples, as is part of the church at Banagher, County Derry (p. 72).

The boundaries of the colony shifted throughout the period, with its greatest extent being in the second half of the thirteenth century, when most of the island was under royal authority. Famine and the 1348–49 plague, however, had a devastating effect and left many manors and villages, which were already suffering depopulation, deserted as settlers died or returned to England. It is also generally agreed that the political instability and turmoil meant building works declined in the fourteenth century. Attempts to halt the Gaelicisation of the colonists by legislation such as the Statutes of Kilkenny in 1369, which outlawed Irish dress, language and intermarriage, failed and Ireland continued to be a drain on the coffers of the English Crown. By the end of the fifteenth century, processes of assimilation, when the powerful 'Old English' (as they later became known) families such as the Butlers became 'more Irish than the Irish themselves' and destruction of settlements by the Gaelic-Irish resulted in the Pale around Dublin being the last stronghold of the Crown. Though the power of the Crown had diminished, Ireland flourished under the 'Old English' lords, the Geraldines. Under their patronage and others, churches and monastic buildings were rebuilt, especially with the addition of towers and cloisters and with door and window alterations. Often the tall, lancet windows of the early Gothic period were replaced with wider limestone tracery windows or smaller ogee-headed windows. The friaries in particular flourished and houses were founded or expanded, especially in the western half of the country, under the patronage of the Gaelic-Irish lords. Examples are the Franciscan friary at Quin, County Clare (p. 58) and Muckross, County Kerry (p. 130). The fifteenth century was also when many of the fortified tower houses were constructed. They were the residences of choice for 'Old English' and Gaelic-Irish lords alike, a good example of which can be found at Derryhivenny, County Galway (p. 118). Some large towers, such as that at Bunratty by the Thomond O'Briens and arguably the finest in the country, were also built.

The main monument types of this period are as follows:

Ringworks are slightly raised circular enclosures with a substantial bank and outer ditch. Evidence for an earlier ringwork was found in excavations of King John's Castle, Limerick (p. 178).

Motte-and-bailey castles consisted of a large, flat-topped mound of earth on which a timber tower was constructed. An earthen enclosure (the bailey) adjoined one side and would have contained kitchens, halls and workshops, etc. St Mullins, County Carlow (p. 40) is a good example.

The great Anglo-Norman stone castles of the thirteenth century can be broadly categorised into three groups: Firstly, castles with towers or keeps, either free-standing or incorporated into the surrounding curtain walls. Trim, County Meath (p. 216) is an example of a rectangular one, though round and polygonal examples also survive (there is a round example in Nenagh, County Tipperary). Secondly, keepless castles such as Limerick (p. 178) and Dublin, which had curtain walls and corner towers but no internal tower. Lastly, towered keeps, which are particular to Ireland, are rectangular keeps with towers at each corner. They were surrounded by curtain walls, Carlow (p. 34) and Ferns, County Wexford, (p. 282) are examples.

Tower houses are single-towered, fortified residences of the 'Old English' and Gaelic-Irish in rural and urban places. They were first built in the fifteenth century (Rathmacknee Castle, County Wexford, p. 286) but examples as late as the seventeenth century can be found (Derryhivenny, County Galway p. 118). Many had associated bawns which do not usually survive.

Town walls are defensive structures surrounding urban areas. Permission (murage grants) from the Crown was necessary to collect taxes in order to pay for their construction. At least fifty-six towns had town walls and all town defences are considered National Monuments. Good examples can be found in Athenry, County Galway and Fethard, County Tipperary.

Abbeys and friaries were constructed, often under the patronage of local rulers, throughout Ireland. European orders such as the Cistercians and Augustinians, who were in Ireland from the 1100s, built their monasteries around a central cloister, with the church usually on the northern side and chapter house, dormitories and refectory on the other sides.

Parish churches are usually very simple structures with little embellishment and are therefore often difficult to date. The organisation of the church into parishes did not really occur until the thirteenth century and in some places the naves of monastic churches were reused. In some of the Anglo-Norman-controlled towns, large parish churches were newly constructed, for example St Mary's in New Ross, County Wexford.

Cathedrals are the principal churches of dioceses and the seat of the bishop. The reforms of the twelfth century saw the creation of four provinces divided into dioceses, each of which required a cathedral. The first half of the thirteenth century saw the building or alteration of many of these cathedrals, such as Cashel, County Tipperary (p. 256) and St Patrick's, Dublin.

Post-Medieval to Modern Ireland (mid sixteenth century – early twentieth century)

The Reformation and the Plantation of Ireland had the biggest effect not only on post-medieval Ireland, but had long-term consequences right up to the present day. The dissolution of the monasteries by Henry VIII resulted in the destruction of monastic establishments and the transfer of Church lands to secular owners. In a bid to control Ireland, Elizabeth I embarked on a campaign of Plantation of loyal English settlers. This was not a success, but after the failed rebellion of Hugh O'Neill and the resultant departure from Ireland in the 1607 Flight of the Earls, large tracts of land were defenceless against colonisation. Under James I/VI loyal English and Scottish Protestants were granted lands, mostly in Ulster and Munster, to the detriment of the native Irish. After the 1641 Rebellion, Cromwell suppressed the Catholic population further by confiscating their land and transplanting them to less-profitable lands west of the Shannon ('to hell or to Connacht') or selling them into slavery in the Caribbean. The land was then granted to soldiers or settled by loyal English Protestants and by 1660, 80 per cent of the land was owned by the new settlers, a situation which remained until the late nineteenth century. The victory of William of Orange over James II's forces in 1691 saw the reintroduction of harsh anti-Catholic laws known as Penal Laws. These laws, which affected non-Anglicans to differing degrees, prevented Catholics from openly practising their religion, holding most public offices and voting and excluded them from the legal profession.

The eighteenth century was a prosperous period with improvements in industry and changes in agriculture. Philosophical and political thinking inspired the French and American Revolutions which had an effect on Irish aspirations for greater political independence. This led to the union of Catholics and Presbyterians in the failed 1798 Rebellion, which resulted in Ireland being ruled directly from London and the Act of Union in 1800. During the eighteenth century, the Anglo-Irish ascendancy, who were the ruling class of the country, built their country seat or 'Big House'. The style and size of these houses varied hugely depending on each builder's taste and income and most were constructed between about 1720 and the Great Famine. Many were designed by the most notable architects of the day with neo-Gothic castles and Classical-influenced designs being the most frequent. As dwellings of the powerful became less fortified, the military function of these buildings was transferred to forts where professional soldiers were garrisoned. From the middle of the sixteenth century, star-shaped forts (Charles Fort, County Cork p. 60) were constructed, influenced by forts on Continental Europe.

Though the Industrial Revolution had some impact on the economy of Ireland, it did not result in the full-scale industrialisation of the country. There was regional specialism such as linen production and shipbuilding but Ireland was predominantly involved in the production of food for export, with an increased demand from the middle of the eighteenth century. Milling, brewing and distilling were the most notable industries, with milling throughout the island and brewing and distilling mostly in urban areas. Some of these industries are still known today, such as Guinness in Dublin, established 1759, and Smithwick's in Kilkenny, the oldest Irish brewery, having been in continuous use since 1710. Milling was important, especially during the Napoleonic Wars, when cereal production was very profitable. Larger-scale windmills were built to cater for demand, especially in the cereal producing regions of counties Down and Wexford. Ballycopeland Windmill in County Down (p. 92) is such an example and processed a variety of grains up to 1915. Reliance on exported agricultural products, however, made the economy vulnerable especially after the ending of the Napoleonic Wars in 1815, when there was a decline in demand. Water power was vital in the milling process though steam power was adopted later and mechanisation continued throughout the nineteenth century. The flax and wool textile industries were predominantly home-produced until the second half of the nineteenth century, but by 1873, the Ulster linen industry was the largest in the world. The mechanisation of the different processes of fibre preparation, spinning, weaving and finishing eventually resulted in the construction of large complexes. A water powered example is preserved at Newmills, County Donegal (p. 90), where corn and flax were processed until 1980.

In 1823, Daniel O'Connell founded the Catholic Association, with the aim of achieving political equality for Catholics and in 1829 won emancipation for Catholics, which allowed them to vote and to enter parliament. The Great Famine had a catastrophic effect on the population of Ireland with 5 million either dying or emigrating between the 1840s and 1914. Landownership had contributed to the Famine and towards the end of the nineteenth century the Land War and The Land Act of 1881 finally improved conditions for tenant farmers. Charles Stewart Parnell and the Home Rule Party then concentrated on gaining home rule for Ireland. The Home Rule Bill was defeated in the House of Lords and was not passed until 1912. With the outbreak of the First World War in 1914 home rule for Ireland, so long fought for, was put on hold.

The main monument types of this period are as follows:

Fortified, semi-fortified and unfortified houses were built with increasing frequency from the early 1600s. These large windowed, multi-storeyed, many-gabled houses usually had a central block with towers at the corners providing flanking defence. Kanturk, County Cork (p. 68), is an unfinished example, while Coppinger's Court (p. 62) in the same county is more defensible. The Elizabethan-style Carrick-on-Suir Castle, County Tipperary (p. 250) is an example of an undefended house. The style of the house was partly dictated by the security of the area and the awareness or desire of the owner to follow current trends. Brick, introduced in the sixteenth century, changed the face of many a town during the seventeenth and eighteenth centuries. One of the early, though unfinished, houses to be built of brick was Jigginstown House, County Kildare (p. 138) started in 1636. The increased use of firearms after 1550 is reflected in architecture by the insertion of musket holes/gun loops (small circular openings) in walls through which small firearms could be discharged. Some can be seen at Ballinafad Castle, County Sligo (p. 236) and Roughan Castle, County Tyrone (p. 264).

Plantation castles were built in the north of the island as a result of the plantation scheme. 'Undertakers' were required to build varying defences depending on the acreage they were granted. The minimum was a bawn. The castles, reflecting where colonists originated, often had Scottish architectural features such as the stepped, round turrets on Monea Castle, County Fermanagh (p. 114).

Follies are ornamental structures built to enhance a garden or view. They can take many forms but the most common are small structures and obelisks, such as Conolly's Folly, County Kildare (p. 136).

Mills housed the machinery for grinding cereals or/and producing textiles. Earlier they were water powered and can be seen close to rivers and streams throughout the country, such as at Newmills, County Donegal (p. 90). Some were also wind-powered such as Tacumshane Windmill, County Wexford (p. 288) and later they used electricity and steam power.

Star-shaped forts were built from the middle of the sixteenth century. They were developed to sustain attack from artillery, which resulted in very wide banks being constructed to absorb the force of cannon fire. Pointed projecting bastions at the corners give the forts their star-shaped appearance. Two very good examples are James Fort (p. 66) and Charles Fort, County Cork (p. 60).

Martello towers were built in the early nineteenth century as artillery posts. They are stout, circular, well-built towers, where soldiers could be garrisoned, with an artillery gun mounted on the roof. About fifty were built along the Irish coast and one at Magilligan Point, County Derry (p. 76), is a good example.

Antrim Round Tower

County Antrim

Map no. 1; GPS: N 54.724025, W 6.208917; Irish Grid: J 15450 87697

Antrim Round Tower, located on the northeast side of Antrim town, in Steeple Park, is all that remains of an ancient monastery. It is thought that it was established by Aodh, a disciple of St Patrick, in the year 495. It was partly destroyed in 1018 and burnt in 1147. The tower itself was built mainly of rough rubble basalt in the tenth or eleventh century. The monastery later became part of the estate of William Clark, who in 1819 removed remains of the monastery buildings, along with a large quantity of human burials. Clark also repaired and restored the tower at this time. In 1822, the tower's conical cap was replaced after it was shattered by a lightning strike. The tower today rises to a height of 28m above ground level and has a circumference of a little over 15m at its base. It originally consisted of three storeys, with access between floors by ladder. The door, which is on the north side, is about 2m above ground level, and at this point the wall is over 1m thick. A block of granite above the door is carved with a cross. There are four windows directly under the roof and a further four windows spaced at different heights around the tower. The Witch's Stone, which is now close to the base of the tower, was originally about 100m further to the north. On its surface are two hollows, which according to legend were created when a witch jumped from the top of the tower and landed on the stone, leaving the impressions of her knee and elbow embedded in the rock.

Clockwise from above: View showing conical cap; View of tower with the Witch's Stone in foreground; View of tower doorway with carved cross above.

Ballymacaldrack Court Tomb

County Antrim

Map no. 2; GPS: N 55.001546, W 6.404536; Irish Grid: D 02144 18284

Ballymacaldrack Court Tomb stands in a fenced-off enclosure about 1km southeast of Dunloy village. Four phases of activity, which continued over several centuries, have been suggested, starting in the early fourth millennium BC with a wooden mortuary structure or excarnation platform (a structure on which bodies were left to decompose), which was burnt. Later, a trench was constructed in the same location by the building up of a cairn. Several men and women were cremated in this trench after which a flagstone floor was inserted. The third phase resulted in the stone structure that is visible today. The tomb, classified as an open court tomb, consists of a flat-topped cairn of stones, with retaining kerbstones on the long sides, and a U-shaped forecourt of eleven upright basalt slabs. From the forecourt, two portal stones mark the entrance into a small stone chamber with a paved floor. The earlier cremation trench/passage, now grassed over, continues behind this chamber for about 6m and is the only example of its kind in Ireland. In the fourth phase the tomb was blocked with stones. The tomb was first excavated by Professor Estyn Evans in 1935. During Evans' excavations, two polished stone axes, said to be 'magic guardians' of the tomb, were found near the chamber entrance amongst the blocking. Evans received so much help from the landowner, Andrew Dooey, that he named the tomb Dooey's Cairn in his honour. The Dooey family presented the tomb to the State in 1975, after which the tomb was again excavated.

Clockwise from top: View of court stones; View from passage to portal tombs; View of cremation trench/passage from northeast.

Bonamargy Friary

County Antrim

Map no. 3; GPS: N 55.202116, W 6.230857; Irish Grid: D 12691 40877

Bonamargy Friary derives its name from its position, at the mouth of the River Margy, on the north coast of County Antrim. The friary buildings consist of a church with north and south ranges and a small gatehouse to the northeast of the church. The west gable of the church is missing and the other buildings survive only in ruins. The early years of the friary are poorly documented; however, it is believed to have been founded by the MacQuillan family for the Franciscan First Order and then transferred to the Third Order around the year 1500. In 1584, a small garrison of English troops was stationed at the friary, where they used the church to stable their horses. A band of MacDonnell Scots attacked the friary and burnt the thatched roof of the church before being driven off by the English. Later the friary was repaired and was used as a base for the Franciscans' missionary work in Scotland. The friary was abandoned at the end of the seventeenth century but continued to be used for burial. Several of the Earls of Ulster are interred in locked vaults, including the celebrated chieftain, Sorley Boy MacDonnell. The Belfast Natural History and Philosophical Society restored and stabilised the friary in 1931 and it was placed in State care by Ballycastle Rural District Council in 1933. The perforated disc-headed cross, just inside the church, is said to mark the grave of Julia McQuillan, the 'black nun' who lived in the friary as a recluse in the mid seventeenth century. According to folklore, she prophesied many events, some of which came true, and others are still outstanding. Her ghost is said to watch over the friary at night.

Clockwise from top: View of friary from east; View of grave marker of Julia McQuillan, the 'black nun'; External view of east window.

Craigs Passage Tomb

County Antrim

Map no. 4; GPS: N 54.993459, W 6.478972; Irish Grid: C 97400 17278

This tomb, known locally as Craigs Dolmen is located in a field close to the edge of a minor road, on the east slopes of the Bann valley. It comprises a capstone, measuring about 2.5m long by 1.7m wide, standing on top of seven upright stones. In 1883, William Gray recorded that the monument had once been covered with earth, with only the capstone visible. Gray's excavations of the tomb revealed a burial urn which probably dated to secondary Bronze Age activity. By 1940, one of the upright stones which supported the capstone had fallen; calamity struck during the winter of 1976, when penetrating water froze along lines of weakness in the capstone shattering it into five pieces. The landowners, the McCaughern family, placed the monument in the guardianship of the Department of the Environment in 1982. The five pieces of the capstone were then removed and repaired with round section steel bar and stone adhesive. The tomb was excavated in May 1985 and at this time the fallen side stone was replaced and the repaired capstone, which weighed 3½ tons, reinstated on top.

Dunluce Castle

County Antrim

Map no. 5; GPS: N 55.211495, W 6.579266; Irish Grid: C 90488 41414

Few castles can boast such a striking and romantic site as that of Dunluce. It is thought that the first castle was built by Richard de Burgh, Earl of Ulster, in the latter part of the thirteenth century but its first definite mention is in 1513, when it was transferred from one branch of the MacQuillan family to another. Subsequently, it passed to the MacDonnell family when Evelyn MacQuillan married Colla MacDonnell. Colla died in 1558 and his younger brother, Sorley Boy, took possession of Dunluce. In 1584, the castle was besieged and taken for a short time by Sir John Perrott until Sorley Boy regained the castle, when a comrade inside the castle hauled the MacDonnell men up the cliff face in a basket. In 1588, the Spanish Armada ship, the *Girona*, struck nearby Lacada Point. Cannons from the wrecked ship were installed in the castle gatehouses, with the rest of the cargo being sold and the funds used by Sorley Boy's son, Randal MacDonnell, first Earl of Antrim, to build a manor house just inside the castle walls. In 1639, during a dinner party, a section of the kitchen collapsed as some of the cliff face gave way. The dinner, kitchen tables, and all the silverware fell into the stormy sea below. Nine of the kitchen staff fell to their deaths and the kitchen boy only survived by clinging to a corner of the crumbling wall. In 1642, the Scottish general Robert Monro, while a guest at Dunluce, arrested his host. The second Earl was then imprisoned at Carrickfergus but escaped and spent the next ten years exiled in England. Following the Restoration of Charles II in 1660, he regained his estates but Dunluce was only occasionally occupied and fell into decay. The Earls of Antrim moved first to Ballymagarry and then to Glenarin Castle. Dunluce came into State guardianship in 1928.

View of manor house from south
showing repaired mullioned windows.

Ballykeel Portal Tomb

County Armagh

Map no. 6; GPS: N 54.131445, W 6.478351; Irish Grid: H 99517 21331

At Ballykeel, a portal tomb, known locally as the Hag's Chair, stands at the southern end of a long rectangular cairn of stones. The portal tomb comprises two portal stones, each about 2m high, divided by a closing stone, and a lower backstone, which together support a massive flat capstone measuring about 3m long by 2.5m wide. Most of the cairn has disappeared and all that remains is a raised rectangular area, covered with grass, with a few stones protruding. It measures about 27m long by 9m wide. At the northern end of the cairn, opposite the portal tomb, there was a stone-lined burial cist, though this is not visible any longer. The tomb was excavated in 1963, at which time the portal tomb was partially collapsed with the backstone split into two pieces. Large quantities of Neolithic pottery sherds were found, mostly in the portal tomb's chamber area. The material found was from at least three highly decorated bowls and a number of other vessels. Many worked flints, including a small javelin head, were also found and though not a trace of bone was discovered, phosphate analysis showed that bones had indeed once been located in the chamber. Their disappearance might be accounted for by high soil acidity, which would have destroyed visible bone. After excavation, the backstone was repaired with bronze dowels and special cement, and then pulled back into its original position. The capstone was then lifted back into position on top of the three supports.

View of portal stones from south.

Ballymacdermot Court Tomb

County Armagh

Map no. 7; GPS: N 54.153689, W 6.371963; Irish Grid: J 06414 23962

Located on the south slope of Ballymacdermot Mountain, this fine court tomb has a D-shaped court, measuring about 7m wide and 5m deep, leading to a 7m-long gallery that is divided into three chambers. The gallery was once roofed by corbelled stones and the entire structure covered with a cairn, although most of this has disappeared, the stones possibly being used for road repairs. In 1815, a local antiquarian, John Bell, and the landowner, Jonathan Seaver, opened the tomb and discovered an urn which contained a substance described as resembling turf mould. What happened to the urn is not recorded, although after his death, Bell's collection of artefacts was purchased by the Royal Society of Antiquaries of Scotland, and it may well be preserved in the National Museum of Scotland, Edinburgh. During the Second World War, the tomb was damaged by an American army tank, which veered off the adjacent road and crashed into the forecourt of the tomb, knocking off the lintel stone and breaking at least three other stones into several pieces. In 1962, the tomb was excavated by a team from Queen's University Belfast. The contents of the burial chambers were found to be much disturbed though some Neolithic pottery sherds, flint flakes and fragments of burnt bone were found. After excavation the broken stones were repaired and fallen stones re-erected.

View of tomb chambers
from southeast

Killevy Churches

County Armagh

Map no. 8; GPS: N 54.137155, W 6.409353; Irish Grid: J 04013 22066

The Killevy Churches are set in a peaceful tree-lined graveyard at the foot of Slieve Gullion. A nunnery was founded here by St Moninna, also known as St Blinne, at the end of the fifth century. It was plundered by Vikings in the year 923 and ravaged by a great storm in 1146, but remained in use as a convent for more than 1,000 years. St Moninna's rule of the monastery was severe. She apparently never looked a man in the face, prayer and vigils were incessant, fasts frequent and all the nuns slept on the hard ground. She died in 518 and a large granite slab in the north of the graveyard is reputed to mark her grave. The date of her death, 6 July, was celebrated into the twentieth century, with pilgrims praying at her grave and at a holy well on the nearby mountainside. Legend relates that when building a new church on the site, the fourth abbess, Derlaisre, found it impossible to carry a long timber down from the mountain to be used as a roof ridge. After spending the night praying to St Moninna for help, the timber was miraculously found next to the church, ready to be installed. The convent was occupied by Augustinian nuns in the Middle Ages, with the last abbess being Alicia O'Hanlon. It was suppressed in 1542, after which the lands were granted to Sir Marmaduke Whitechurche. The long narrow structure on the site today is the remains of two churches, later joined by connecting walls. The west church has a massive lintelled door, probably surviving from an earlier church on the site. The east church, with a steeply pitched east gable and large window, probably dates from the fifteenth century. A round tower formerly stood near the church but it was blown down in a gale about 1768.

Clockwise from top left: Interior view of western door of west church; View of St Moninna's grave; Exterior view of western door of west church showing massive lintel above door.

Kilnasaggart Pillar Stone

County Armagh

Map no. 9; GPS: N 54.072264, W 6.378937; Irish Grid: J 06166 14889

The Kilnasaggart Pillar Stone is located in a modern enclosure in the middle of a field, about 2km south of Jonesborough. It stands over 2m high and is one of the earliest historically dateable stone monuments in Ireland. It bears the old Irish inscription: '*IN LOC SO TANI MMAIRNI TERNOCH MACCERAN BIC ER CUL PETER AP STEL*', which translates as 'This place, Ternoc, son of Ciaran the Little, bequeathed it under the protection of the Apostle Peter.' Ternoc's death is recorded in the Annals of Tighearnach as AD 716, hence the pillar can be dated to about the year 700. On the face of the stone, above and below the inscription, are two carved crosses, one plain and another enclosed in a circle. On the back of the stone there are at least ten more crosses, of which the three in a line down the middle of the stone are larger and more refined, with their arms turning off in curving spirals. Beneath the circles are thirty-one incised strokes, believed to be marks from sharpening knives or swords. The name *Kil-na-saggart* signifies 'Church of the Priests'. A 1609 map indicates a roofless church in the area, though evidence of this has not survived. A description of the location by Mr Reade in 1856, records the cross at the northern edge of an unusual circular burial ground, with the graves placed in two concentric circles, such that the feet of the dead pointed towards a small pillar stone at the centre. Traces of this layout cannot be found today and excavations in the 1960s uncovered an early Christian cemetery, with the graves all lying in the usual east–west direction.

Left: View of stone from north.
Top: View of inscription recording Ternoc,
son of Ciaran the Little.
Above: View of plain inscribed cross.

Navan Fort

County Armagh

Map no. 10; GPS: N 54.348153, W 6.697969; Irish Grid: H 84717 45165

About 2.5km west of the city of Armagh is the legendary ancient capital of the kingdom of Ulster, *Emain Macha*, known today as Navan Fort. The site is part of a large archaeological complex known as the Navan complex, which includes Haughey's Fort and King's Stables. A wide, circular, V-shaped ditch with a massive external bank of earth encloses the hilltop and measures about 286m in overall diameter. On its summit, a grassy flat-topped mound about 50m in diameter rises to a height of 6m. To the southeast is a 30m-diameter ring-barrow. The mound was excavated in the 1960s, revealing a complex sequence of Early Iron Age features. A series of figure-of-eight structures was thought to represent the rebuilding of a circular house and yard, but present thinking is that they might have been open-air structures for ritual. Much larger unroofed figure-of-eight structures have been found in the area of the ring-barrow. One of the artefacts found in the excavation was the skull of a Barbary ape. This exotic animal is thought to have been a gift originating in North Africa, and presented to an Ulster king about 390–20 BC. About 100 BC the area was cleared and a 40m-diameter wooden structure erected, comprising more than 275 posts arranged in five concentric rings with a western entrance. A massive 12m-high pole stood at its centre, the stump of which was still preserved in the soil and dated by dendrochronology to 95 BC. The wooden structure was then filled with limestone boulders to form a cairn 2.8m high, and set on fire. When the flames died down, the remaining structure was covered with a mound of carefully layered turf and soil. The purpose of the structure and its apparent ritual destruction can only be guessed at.

Clockwise from above: View of mound from east; View of outer earthwork; View of bank which surrounds the central mound.

Ballyloughan Castle

County Carlow

Map no. 11; GPS: N 52.673025, W 6.898363; Irish Grid: S 74570 58511

Ballyloughan Castle is located 4 miles east of Muine Beag and although there is not a record of the construction of the castle, or of its early history, its style indicates that it was built in the thirteenth century. It consisted of a rectangular courtyard, about 46m square, surrounded by a high, 1.5m-wide curtain wall. The wall was protected by two rectangular corner towers, one at the northeast and one at the southwest. One of these towers was converted into a small gabled cottage during the eighteenth century, and later abandoned. Access to the courtyard interior was controlled by a gatehouse with two circular three-storey towers, flanking an arched entranceway. Part of the castle's 3m-wide and 1m-deep moat was found in excavations carried out in 1955. It was filled with water from a nearby lake, from which the castle derives its name, *Baile an Lochain*, or 'town of the small lake'. When the lake dried out, the moat was subsequently filled in. During the fourteenth century, Ballyloughan was occupied by the MacMurrough Kavanaghs, who had control over most of County Carlow. Bryan Mac Donagh Kavanagh was at

Ballyloughan in 1603 and the Kavanaghs continued in residence until 1641. After the Cromwellian conquest of Ireland, the Ballyloughan lands were granted to Lord Chief Baron Bysshe, Dudley Bagnall and John Beauchamp. Beauchamp built the house on the hill-slope behind the castle, reusing some of the cut stonework from the castle. His family continued to reside here into the eighteenth century. This house, however, also subsequently fell into ruin. A local story relates that a crock of gold still lies buried somewhere in the castle grounds.

Clockwise from above: View to gatehouse with remains of curtain wall in fore and middle ground; View of gatehouse mural stairway; View upwards in gatehouse tower.

Browneshill Portal Tomb

County Carlow

Map no. 12; GPS: N 52.837553, W 6.8811; Irish Grid: S 75453 76838

Browneshill Portal Tomb lies about 3km east of Carlow town, just off the R726 Carlow-to-Baltinglass road. The tomb's massive granite capstone measures about 4.7m by 6.1m and is 2m thick. It is estimated to weigh over 100 tonnes, making it the largest of its kind in Europe. The chamber faces east, with the eastern end of the capstone supported by two portal stones and a door stone, and the western end resting on low backstones. Its construction dates from the Neolithic period, *c.* 3000 BC. Originally the tomb might have been set in a mound with a burial located in the chamber under the capstone. Owing to its immense size, the capstone would have required the efforts of several hundred people to set it in position. This is probably also why it has never been excavated.

Carlow Castle

County Carlow

Map no. 13; GPS: N 52.836243, W 6.935956; Irish Grid: S 71758 76636

The remains of Carlow Castle are located near the centre of Carlow town. The first defensive structure on the site was built out of timber about the year 1180, by Hugh de Lacy for John de Clahull. The next stage of construction was begun about 1210 by William Marshal, Lord of Leinster, and saw the erection of a three-storey tower with circular towers at each corner. Its walls were more than 2m thick. The tower would have been surrounded by a curtain wall enclosing associated buildings, although no evidence survives today. The castle was part of Marshal's plan to create a strong market town on the banks of the River Barrow which could trade downriver to New Ross. In 1494, it was attacked and seized by James Fitzgerald of Kildare. It was then attacked by Silken Thomas in 1534, Rory Oge O'Moore in 1577, Sir Morgan Kavanagh in 1641 and Thomas Preston in 1646. Finally in 1650, Oliver Cromwell and his son-in-law, General Ireton, attacked and left the castle in ruins. Drawings made in the eighteenth century show the castle still standing in reasonable condition. In 1814, however, it was leased to Dr

Philip Parry Middleton who had the intention of converting the castle for use as a lunatic asylum. The heavy stone vaults presented something of an obstacle to his plans and a speedy remedy was adopted of drilling into the walls and loading them with blasting powder, which was then detonated. The total collapse of the eastern half of the castle came one Sunday morning when most of the local population was in church. Apparently the dreadful crash caused them to dive for cover under the church pews. It was said that if his asylum had been successful then the first lunatic to be admitted should have been Dr Middleton himself.

Clockwise from above:
Interior view of the castle's west wall; View into round tower; Exterior view of surviving castle walls showing batter.

St Mullins Monastic Settlement

County Carlow

Map no. 14; GPS: N 52.489268, W 6.928554; Irish Grid: S 72831 38032

A monastic settlement was founded here by St Moling, and the name, St Mullins, derives from a corruption of his name. Legend relates that he chose the site after casting a net into the River Barrow, and producing a miraculous catch of salmon. The river also allowed easy access to his companions, St Lazerian, who was upriver at Leighlinbridge, and St Abbanus, who was downriver at New Ross. According to the legend, the first structure on the site, an oratory, was built for St Moling by the great architect Gobán Saor, using wood from the sacred *Eó Ruis* yew tree. St Moling later added a mill and watercourse which were built with his own hands and took eight years to complete. The path of the watercourse can be seen to this day. St Moling died in 696 and is said to be buried under his oratory. Inside the enclosure, the church on the left-hand side (at the north) is a Church of Ireland church built in 1811 and now used as a heritage centre. The next building is a church known as *Teampall Mór*, which dates to the fifteenth century. Adjacent are the remains of what is known as St Mullin's Abbey and the stump of a round tower. Beyond the tower is an oratory which serves as a mausoleum for the Kavanagh family, descendants of the Kings of Leinster. A domestic building or a possible rare, late-seventeenth- or early-eighteenth-century Catholic church stands next to this mausoleum. Behind the abbey there is a small oratory measuring little more than 2m square and the remains of a high cross. A well-preserved Norman motte and bailey can be seen just outside the church enclosure, with St Moling's Holy Well in the valley below.

Clockwise from above: Anglo-Norman motte and bailey just outside the church enclosure; View of St Moling's Holy Well; View of remains of round tower.

Clogh Oughter Castle

County Cavan

Map no. 15; GPS: N 54.018259, W 7.462034; Irish Grid: H 35312 07795

The round Clogh Oughter Castle stands on a small rocky island in Lough Oughter, about 300m from the shoreline. Its construction was started by the Anglo-Norman, William Gorm de Lacy. The castle had reached a height of only two storeys before William Gorm died in 1233. The O'Reilly clan then seized the castle and it was raised to a height of five storeys during their occupation, which lasted almost continuously until the first part of the seventeenth century. In 1369, the castle served as a gloomy prison for Philip O'Reilly, who was held captive for several years by his own brothers with only a meagre ration of oats and a cup of water a day. Apparently Philip survived only by drinking his own urine. During the Plantation of Ulster, in 1610, it was designated a royal castle and Captain Hugh Hume was appointed its constable. On the first day of the 1641 Rebellion, the O'Reillys attacked and retook the castle. Captain Hume was taken prisoner and was soon joined by the old Bishop of Kilmore, William Bedell, and his two sons. The men were held in chains in a cold, wet and windy room at the top of the tower. They were released in January 1642. Bedell died from fever a few days later, evidently suffering from the effects of being held in the castle. In 1653, the castle became the last stronghold to fall in the Cromwellian Wars. It was attacked by Cromwell from three sides before the walls were eventually blown up by a massive explosion of gunpowder. When it was excavated in 1987, the grim remains of four human skeletons were discovered, all possibly casualties of the final fatal siege of 1653.

View of castle from north, showing entrance at a height of about 4.5m.

Cohaw Court Tomb

County Cavan

Map no. 16; GPS: N 54.057373, W 7.018719; Irish Grid: H 64310 12461

Cohaw is a fine example of a dual court tomb. It has a north–south alignment and measures about 25m in length and 13m in width. A court at each end opens on to a 15m-long gallery of two chambers at each end, with a central fifth chamber. The court at the northern end is U-shaped and appears to have been closed off by four posts and a packed earth wall, with a gap in the middle. The court at the southern end is semicircular and was probably closed off by a post fence. Excavations in 1949 revealed a young male human skull, cremated human bone, human teeth and a single Neolithic pottery bowl. Construction of the tomb appears to have started with the building of the central chamber, in which a youth's teeth had been deposited. The gallery walls were then extended, with another two chambers added on either side of the central chamber. The roof was probably made of capstones, though none of these remain. Cavan County Council roadmen used some of the stones in the construction of the nearby road, with the owner of the land receiving a small payment in compensation in the 1940s. Some of the missing stones were also built into the structure of the new Cootehill church.

View of southern chambers.

Drumlane Church and Round Tower

County Cavan

Map no. 17; GPS: N 54.059287, W 7.477956; Irish Grid: H 34235 12354

The first monastic settlement at Drumlane was founded by St Mogue at the end of the sixth century. In the middle of the twelfth century the site was taken over by the Augustinians, who founded St Mary's Priory. The priory was probably destroyed just after the dissolution of the monasteries and the earliest surviving feature on the site is the 14m-high stub of a round tower. The diameter at the base of the tower is about 16m and the walls are nearly 1.5m thick. On its north face, approximately level with the door, are two much-weathered carvings of birds, said to be a cock and a hen. The church, which stands next to the tower, probably originates from the late thirteenth century, but was altered with the insertion of late-medieval tracery and plain windows. The buttresses and probably the whole western section of the church are early seventeenth century with the medieval west door being reused, most likely from the destroyed priory. Legend tells of an underground passage which ran from the church for a few hundred metres south to the priory. The *Breac Maedoc*, a small shrine in the shape of an ancient church, which held relics of Saints Laurence, Mark and Stephen, was kept at Drumlane from the time of St Mogue. In 1846, it was borrowed from the Drumlane parish priest and subsequently sold to a Dublin jeweller. It was brought by the antiquarian, Dr Petrie, and presented to the National Museum in Dublin in the 1890s.

Above (l–r): View into the church through the west door; View of round tower from the south; View through Gothic church windows.
Below: View of site from north.

Brian Boru's Fort

County Clare

Map no. 18; GPS: N 52.819104, W 8.452778; Irish Grid: R 69523 74293

Brian Boru's Fort, also known as Béal Boru, stands in a serene setting overlooking Lough Derg about 2km north of Killaloe. The site is traditionally associated with Brian, High King of Ireland and founder of the O'Brien dynasty, who died fighting the Vikings at the Battle of Clontarf in the year 1014. Excavation in 1962 revealed two phases of use: the earliest, a ringfort which had been occupied in the eleventh century, and a later phase of an immense bank, raised central area and ditch that are likely to be the results of an attempt to construct a motte or ringwork. It is this unfinished phase that can be seen on the site today. It was probably built by the Anglo-Normans in 1207, as suggested by the Annals of Clonmacnoise: 'The English of Meath and Leinster with their forces went to Killaloe to build a castle there, near the Borowe, and were frustrated of their purpose, did neither castle nor other thing worthy of memory, but lost some men and horses in theire jorney, and soe returned to their houses back again'. The earlier ringfort had a substantial bank up to 5.7m thick, faced with stone on the inside and with a wooden palisade on the outer face. A rectangular post-built house, partially paved with well-worn local slate, was located in the interior, in which a Hiberno-Norse coin and a slate motif piece were found. This phase of use was probably ended by Turlough O'Connor, King of Connacht, who raided and burnt Béal Boru and the nearby O'Brien stronghold at Kincora in 1116. When Murtagh O'Brien died in 1119, Turlough ended the O'Brien supremacy by again raiding Kincora, apparently throwing the stones and timber of Brian's great palace into the waters of the Shannon.

View from top of fort into
neighbouring forest.

Corcomroe Abbey

County Clare

Map no. 19; GPS: N 53.126908, W 9.054065; Irish Grid: M 29489 08972

The Cistercian Abbey of Corcomroe, Santa Maria de Petra Fertili (St Mary of the fertile rock) stands in a fertile valley amongst the grey, stony Burren hills. Though several dates have been suggested for its founding it was most likely about the year 1194. The abbey plan for the most part conforms to the established Cistercian norms. The church is well preserved but most of the cloister buildings have not survived. The original nave-and-chancel church, with transepts and aisles, was divided by the insertion of a tower in the fifteenth century. The chancel is lit by three lancet windows and a single light above. Some capitals are beautifully decorated with stylised foliage, flowers and human heads. The highest quality workmanship can be found in the Romanesque-influenced rib-vaulted chancel. Externally the chancel is decorated with string courses and shafts at the building angles where the lower terminus of the upper shaft ends in a dragon's head which grips the string course with its teeth. Internally, on the northern side of the chancel, in a tomb niche, lies the effigy of Conor na Siudaine O'Brien, King of Munster, who was slain in a nearby battle in 1267. It shows him crowned and wearing a long, pleated robe and pointed shoes. This is one of only two royal effigies known to exist in Ireland, the other being that of Felim O'Connor, King of Connacht, in Roscommon Friary (p. 234). The north side of the chancel also houses a decorated sedilia and a carving of a bishop. On the opposite wall is another decorated niche. After dissolution, in 1554, the abbey was granted to Murrough O'Brien, Earl of Thomond. A community, however, resided here until 1628, when Father John O'Dea, a Cistercian from the Irish College at Salamanca was named as abbot.

Left: View west from rib-vaulted chancel. (Note original floor level in excavated areas at pillar bases.)
Right: View to nave west windows and door.

COUNTY CLARE: CORCOMROE ABBEY　51

Dysert O'Dea

County Clare

Map no. 20; GPS: N 52.909226, W 9.068452; Irish Grid: R 28165 84761

A monastic settlement was founded here by St Tola in the first part of the eighth century. On the site today can be seen the remains of a twelfth-century church, a round tower, and in the adjoining field a cross from the twelfth-century reform period. The cross, which greets approaching visitors, depicts the Crucifixion and a bishop in bold relief on the western side, with the other sides decorated with animal interlace among other motifs. Scenes carved on three sides of the sloping base are thought to depict Adam and Eve, Daniel in the Lions' Den and a foundation ceremony. Crowning the cross, the shrine-like top was once removable, and was an infallible cure for toothache. The cross fell twice, being re-erected by Michael O'Dea in 1683 and by Francis Synge in 1871. The church has been altered many times in its history and shows evidence of several phases. The beautiful twelfth-century Romanesque doorway in the southern wall of the church has four orders, all decorated differently, with twelve human heads interspersed with fantastical creatures depicted on the outer order. The human heads seem to depict individuals and show a variety of hairstyles and facial hair. A local legend recounts the tale of how Dysert O'Dea acquired its round tower. The tower was said to have originated from nearby Rath Blathmac but St Manawla or Bánála hoisted it on her shoulders and stole it when the holy man of Rath slept. On being discovered she threw the tower to Dysert, where it stuck broken topped, as may be seen to this day. Bánála is the local name for the founding saint, St Tola of Clonard, and is a corruption of the local name for the Dysert O'Dea cross, which is the white cross of Tola (*Cros-bhán-Thola*).

Clockwise from top left:
View of remains of round tower; Close-up view of heads in outer order of Romanesque door; External view of magnificent Romanesque door in south wall; View of site from south.

Leamaneh Castle

County Clare

Map no. 21; GPS: N 52.987717, W 9.139863; Irish Grid: R 23499 93570

Leamaneh Castle comprises a fifteenth-century tower house, extended in the seventeenth century with the addition of a large manor house. The tower house was built about 1480, probably by Turlogh O'Brien. It contains five storeys of small chambers, all lit by narrow defensive loops, and accessed by a spiral staircase. In 1543, Turlogh's son, Murrough, pledged his allegiance to the English Crown and was created the first Earl of Thomond and Baron Inchiquin. In 1648, a descendant, Conor O'Brien, and his wife, Mary McMahon (Máire Rua or Red Mary, on account of her flame-red hair), extended the tower with the addition of a large four-storey gabled house. In stark contrast to the earlier tower, the house has large mullioned and transomed windows which ensured the rooms were bright and airy, indicating its occupants were less concerned about security and more interested in comfort. Conor's time at Leamaneh was, however, short-lived as he was killed by Cromwell's soldiers just three years after its completion. His son, Donagh, was the last of the O'Briens to live at Leamaneh. At the end of the seventeenth century he moved the family seat to Dromoland Castle, County Clare. In about 1908, the gateway to the courtyard

of Leamaneh was re-erected in the gardens of Dromoland where it can still be seen. There are many stories about Máire Rua, who was evidently a formidable character. Most are a combination of historical legend and myth. One story tells of her numerous husbands, many of whom met their deaths with a push from one of the upper castle windows. Another story tells that to put an end to her mischief, locals sealed her up in a hollow tree trunk.

Top: Interior view of manor house extension. **Above left:** Interior view of southern wall of manor house. **Above right:** View of Leamaneh gateway, now located at Dromoland Castle.

Poulnabrone Portal Tomb

County Clare

Map no. 22; GPS: N 53.048695, W 9.140046; Irish Grid: M 23595 00356

Poulnabrone Portal Tomb, an iconic symbol of the Burren, stands proudly on a limestone pavement close to the Corofin-to-Ballyvaughan road. Generations of locals and tourists alike have been photographed beneath its large capstone. It was built as a territorial marker at a time when the communities were large enough to have to compete for resources with other groups. In 1985 a crack in the eastern portal stone necessitated the conservation and excavation of the monument which resulted in the replacement of one sidestone and the insertion of another to help support the capstone. During the excavation the disarticulated remains of at least twenty-one people, bone, stone artefacts, pottery fragments and animal bone were excavated from the chamber. Radiocarbon dating showed that the bones had a 600-year date range from 3800–3200 BC. These people, sixteen adults and five children, had decomposed elsewhere and their bones were then gathered and placed in the tomb in a single act sometime after 3200 BC. It is likely that they were interred at the time the tomb was constructed. The bones themselves tell a more personal story. Arthritis was common, especially in the neck and shoulders, and the children had suffered malnutrition or infectious diseases. The tip of a projectile point was found in the hip bone of an individual and, although the wound did not cause his/her death, it occurred at the same time. It seems that the capstone of the tomb was always intended to be visible and the low cairn, in which it stands, intended only to support the orthostats. A large flat stone lies adjacent to the low end of the monument and it seems it fell into this position when, around 1840, a Mr Patrick Davoren's uncle was showing his strength by lifting the capstone.

View of tomb from east.

Quin Friary

County Clare

Map no. 23; GPS: N 52.819279, W 8.863006; Irish Grid: R 41866 74566

The well-preserved fifteenth-century friary at Quin is located on a green plain close to a stream called Rine. It was built on and within the ruins of the four-towered Anglo-Norman castle built by Thomas de Clare *c.* 1280. There is some confusion as to the date of its founding but it seems most likely that it was constructed around 1433, when Pope Eugenius IV granted a licence to Maccon MacNamara for the foundation of a friary of Franciscans. The remains consist of a nave-and-chancel church with a south transept off the nave and tower and domestic buildings including a toilet block reached by a bridge. The southern wall and part of the eastern and western walls of the church are unusually thick as the builders used the castle's curtain walls. The east window of the church is a three-light, switch-line tracery window and there are many examples of other Gothic windows of various forms. The cloister walkways are vaulted and arcaded with the openings set in pairs between high buttresses. In 1541, the friary was dissolved and granted to Connor O'Brien, the third Earl of Thomond. Subsequently it passed through many hands but as late as 1681 friars still inhabited its buildings. They were finally expelled by Colonels William and Henry Stamer, two brothers, who set fire to the abbey. The friars sought refuge a few kilometres northwest of Quin, at Drim, County Clare. The last friar, John Hogan, died in 1820, aged eighty, and his grave can be found in the friary's east cloister walk today.

Clockwise from top:
View of refectory;
View of friary from south;
View of cloister walkway
and arcading.

Charles Fort

County Cork

Map no. 24; GPS: N 51.698776, W 8.499663; Irish Grid: W 65503 49649

Around 1677, the Duke of Ormonde initiated the construction of a new fort for the defence of Kinsale town and harbour against a possible French invasion. The new fort, built at a cost of over £70,000, was named Charles Fort, after King Charles II. It was designed by Sir William Robinson, the Surveyor General of Ireland, and is recognised as being one of the finest examples of a pentagonal bastion fort. The two bastions facing the sea are called Devil's Bastion and Charles' Bastion and are still a formidable sight for a sailor approaching the harbour. The other three landward-facing bastions are known as North, Cockpit and Flagstaff Bastions. Charles Fort remained an army barracks until the formation of the Irish Free State in 1922. During the Irish Civil War it was burned and partially destroyed by the retreating anti-Treaty forces. One of the early governors of the fort, Colonel Warender, had a daughter named Wilful, who became engaged to a member of the fort's garrison, Sir Trevor Ashurst. On the evening of their wedding, she commented on some flowers on the rocks below the steep battlements. Ashurst sent a young guard down to get the flowers, swapping places in the sentry box as the guard scrambled down the rocks. Ashurst soon dozed off and was unfortunately discovered sleeping on duty by his father-in-law, the Governor, who shot him on the spot, unaware that it was his son-in-law who had traded places with the sentry. When the young bride heard of the tragedy, she flung herself onto the rocks below the battlements. Her ghost, known locally as 'The White Lady', is still said to haunt the fort's towering walls.

View of fort from Charles bastion showing officers' quarters in middle ground.

View from Devil's Bastion to harbour entrance.

Coppinger's Court

County Cork

Map no. 25; GPS: N 51.571668, W 9.067036; Irish Grid: W 26069 35928

In 1621, Sir Walter Coppinger built Ballyverine Castle, more commonly known as Coppinger's Court, in the Rowry Valley between Rosscarberry and Glandore in County Cork. Coppinger's Court was a four-storey house with a central structure flanked by fortified towers. In its day it was the largest house in Carberry. According to an exaggerated tradition, the house had a chimney for every month, a door for every week and a window for every day in the year. The octagonal chimney stacks and turrets are still well preserved. Sir Walter had been settled at Baltimore but after quarrelling with Sir Fineen O'Driscoll he left to set up a new and finer town at Ballyverine. His plans for converting the Rowry River into a canal and the development of a new market town, however, came to nothing. Sir Walter was said to be an incredibly cruel and tyrannical lord who ruled over the local peasantry with an iron fist. A story relates that gallows were set up on a beam that projected from the house, where victims of his cruelty were hanged by the neck. Other stories tell of a dark dungeon basement where his prisoners were chained up in misery for years on end. Sir Walter died in 1639, apparently struck down by some divine power in retribution for all his wicked deeds. The house was burnt down in the 1641 Rebellion and in 1700 Sir Walter's descendants lost their estates when outlawed for high treason.

Interior view looking east.

Drombeg Stone Circle and Fulachta Fia

County Cork

Map no. 26; GPS: N 51.564599, W 9.087195; Irish Grid: W 24660 35162

Situated in the rolling countryside of west Cork, Drombeg is the finest of a number of stone circles in County Cork. There are seventeen stones in the circle, of which thirteen are the original stones. The stone at the northwest, opposite the circle entrance, lies horizontally and gives the circle its alias 'The Druid's Altar'. When viewed from the circle entrance, this horizontal stone aligns with the setting position of the sun during the midwinter solstice on 21 December. This celestial alignment was first noted by Boyle Somerville in 1923. Excavations in 1958, prior to restoration, revealed that the entire inner area of the circle was covered with a gravelled floor around 10cm thick. A broken pot was discovered at the centre of the circle which contained the cremated remains of a young adolescent. Other artefacts found included eighty other smashed sherds, four bits of shale and sweepings from a pyre. To the west of the circle are the remains of two connected round stone-built huts and a *fulachta fia* or burnt-stone mound. *Fulachtaí fia* were used by placing heated stones in a water-filled trough to produce hot water. The traditional theory is that they were used to cook meat but other suggestions are that they could have been used for activities such as bathing, dyeing, tanning or even brewing. In August 2007, two Galway-based archaeologists experimented by adding heated stones and barley to a large wooden trough. After a period of time the liquor was transferred to another vessel with the addition of yeast and wild plant flavours. After allowing a few days for fermentation, the 300 litres of water were transformed into palatable frothy ale.

Above: View into circle over recumbent stone.
Left: Remains of *fulachta fia*. (Note water-filled trough at centre and penannular stone bank.)

James Fort

County Cork

Map no. 27; GPS: N 51.699481, W 8.510456; Irish Grid: W 64757 49733

Construction of James Fort, named after King James I/VI, began in 1602, immediately after the Battle of Kinsale. The fort, designed by the engineer Paul Ive and built on the site of an earlier fortification, was finished in 1607. It is pentagonal, with earthen bastions on the corners. At the centre of the earthworks is a rectangular stone bawn, which has recently been repaired. The bawn surrounds a tower and other outbuildings. A tunnel and trench run down to the blockhouse, by the water's edge. Underwater chains were run from the blockhouse across to Charles Fort on the opposite side of the harbour entrance, blocking the passage of enemy ships. After the construction of Charles Fort, James Fort became known as Old Fort and Charles Fort, New Fort. On 2 October 1690, during the Williamite–Jacobite War, the Earl of Marlborough attempted to take the town of Kinsale from the Irish Jacobite forces. James Fort was defended by the Governor Colonel Cornelius O'Driscoll and a garrison of 450 men. During the early stages of the battle an explosion in the gunpowder magazine killed forty of O'Driscoll's men, and the walls were quickly scaled by the invaders. A further 200 of O'Driscoll's men were slain in the ensuing battle with the remainder of the garrison being taken as prisoners by the Williamite forces.

View of block house at water's edge.

Kanturk Castle

County Cork

Map no. 28; GPS: N 52.163877, W 8.903561; Irish Grid: R 38220 01668

It is thought that MacDonogh MacCarthy, Lord of Duhallow, began building Kanturk Castle at the start of the seventeenth century. The castle measures about 28m long by 11m wide and comprises a central four-storey block, with a five-storey 28m-high tower placed at each corner. The mullioned windows, hood mouldings, cornices, quoins, corbel stones, fireplaces and doors were all made of cut limestone. One legend relates that a team of seven stonemasons, all named John, were employed in its construction. Hence it was known as *Carrig-na-Shane-Saor*, or The Rock of John the Mason. Another legend tells that the labourers were driven so hard that some dropped dead from exhaustion, and their blood was then used to bind the castle's mortar. MacCarthy's stepbrother, McAuliffe, gifted with second sight, said of the castle, ''Tis too good for the crows to live in, and it will never be finished.' The castle was built as a defence against the English and as news of its massive fortification reached the Privy Council, orders were placed that all construction should cease. Whether the castle was ever completed remains an open question. In 1632, the castle was mortgaged to Sir Philip Percival. Following the MacCarthy involvement in the 1641 Rebellion, it passed directly into the hands of Sir Percival, whose descendants were later created Earls of Egmont. They held the castle until 1900, when the Countess of Egmont gifted the castle to the National Trust. In 1951 the National Trust gave a 1,000-year lease to An Taisce for the rent of one shilling per year, but also gave £500 annually for its upkeep. It was later placed in the care of the OPW and in 1998 its title deeds transferred to An Taisce, in trust for the people of Ireland.

Clockwise from top:
View of castle interior;
View of castle interior. (Note fine fireplace on first floor.);
View of the fine Renaissance-style entrance doorway on the northwest side of the building.

Ballybriest Court Tomb

County Derry

Map no. 29; GPS: N 54.739339, W 6.816845; Irish Grid: H 76254 88572

Ballybriest Court Tomb is located about 5km northwest of Cookstown. It is a dual court tomb, with 4.5m-long forecourts at both ends and galleries about 6m long, back to back, but on not quite the same axis. During the early nineteenth century, the tomb was on the land of Samuel Wright, an industrious and improving landowner, who unfortunately removed some of the stones for building material. The north horns of both cairns are no longer present and most of the south side of the east gallery has also disappeared. In 1934, the tomb was placed into State guardianship under the Land Purchase Commission. At this time it was so overgrown that little of its structure could be made out. In June 1937, the tomb was subsequently excavated and preserved. Considerable quantities of potsherds, cremated human bone and finely worked flints were discovered. Charcoal was also found which was identified by the Royal Botanic Gardens, Edinburgh, as hazel, oak, gorse and willow. A local story relates that in the early 1900s, turf cutters who were working close to the tomb revealed a pair of ancient slippers, a bronze sword and a pot containing cremated remains. Sadly, there is no record of what happened to these discoveries.

View from western gallery interior.

Banagher Church

County Derry

Map no. 30; GPS: N 54.902561, W 6.947608; Irish Grid: C 67559 06607

Banagher Church was reputedly founded by St Muiredhach O'Heney in the eleventh century. Tradition relates that the church was first built about a kilometre away, but then mysteriously moved to the present location in the dead of night. Muiredhach was then led to the new location by a stag that carried the saint's holy books on his antlers. The earliest part of the church is the nave, with the style of the west door indicating a date of the first half of the twelfth century. The chancel was added in the early thirteenth century and a beautiful transitional or 'School of the West' style window is preserved in the southern wall. The date that the church fell into disuse is not recorded, but in 1622 it was reported as already in ruins. About 1794, Colonel Carey of Dungiven Castle, excavated the church using crowbars and pickaxes in search of buried treasure. Only a few stone objects were found and the excavated material was replaced to its original height. The site was placed into State care in 1880 and restoration work was carried out a few years later. It was also excavated and repaired in 1972 with the built-up soil being then removed from the south, east and west walls. It is thought the ruined building just outside the church gate was a residence and that Muiredhach used to appear to the people from the high doorway. A twelfth- or early-thirteenth-century mortuary house just southeast of the church is said to be the burial place of Muiredhach and the sand surrounding the tomb is thought to be sacred. Legend says that, in any horse race, whoever can throw the Banagher sand on the rider as he passes ensures victory for that horse.

Above (l–r): Interior and exterior views of transitional or 'School of the West' window in south wall of chancel; View through west door into church. **Below:** View of mortuary house, said to be the burial place of St Muiredhach.

Dungiven Priory

County Derry

Map no. 31; GPS: N 54.917425, W 6.921687; Irish Grid: C 69196 08287

According to tradition, St Neachtain founded a monastery at Dungiven in the seventh century. This was succeeded by a twelfth-century Augustinian priory, which is associated with the O'Cahan family. Cooey O'Cahan died in 1385 and is buried inside the very fine tomb located on the south side of the (fenced-off) chancel. The tomb is decorated with the sculptured Cooey lying recumbent with one hand on his sword. On the front face of the tomb, six gallowglasses can be seen, sculptured in relief. The tomb has been much restored after suffering several injuries. One story goes that a regiment of Scottish Highlanders took offence at Cooey's nickname, *Cooey na Gall,* or 'Terror of the Foreigners' and broke off some of the figures on the front of the tomb. Around the time of Cooey's death, the church was desecrated and left to fall into decay. It was restored and reconsecrated by the Archbishop of Armagh in 1397 and then occupied by the Augustinian canons until the dissolution of the monasteries. In the seventeenth century, the church was converted for Protestant worship. Around this time Sir Edward Doddington, an English soldier, added a manor house and bawn to the tower which stood at the west of the nave. The tower

collapsed into the nave in 1784 and all that remains of the manor house are the foundation walls which can still be seen just southwest of the church. Around 1720, a new church was built in Dungiven town, which reused the roof timbers from the old priory church. The priory was then abandoned and fell into ruin. It was excavated in 1982 and shortly after this a roof was put on the chancel and the gates installed to protect Cooey's tomb from further damage.

Clockwise from far left: View of church nave looking east to closed chancel; Cooey O'Cahan's tomb in the chancel; View of site from east.

Magilligan Point Martello Tower

County Derry

Map no. 32; GPS: N 55.191731, W 6.961555; Irish Grid: C 66186 38785

The Martello tower at Magilligan Point, built in 1812 by Henry, Mullins and McMahon Building Contractors, was one of the last of many Martello towers to be built in Ireland. It protected the approaches to the City of Derry. The Martello towers owe their origin to the wars following the French revolution. On the 7th February 1794, two British warships unsuccessfully attacked a tower at Mortella Point, Corsica. This tower proved impregnable from the seaward side but was eventually taken by a land based force. The British consequently copied the design of the tower but due to a linguistic mix-up, got the name wrong, misspelling Mortella as Martello. By the end of the Napoleonic Wars, Martello towers had spread as far as the East Indies and Canada, with fifty towers, all individually numbered, being built around the Irish coast. The tower at Magilligan Point is built of dressed stone. It stands 10m high and measures 12m in diameter. The doorway, at first floor level, could be defended from above by a large machicolated musketry position. Inside the doorway a large domed room is divided by a curving wall, this would have been the home for one officer and about twenty-four men. A stairway leads down to the magazine and storeroom, below which a basement could be accessed by a trapdoor. On the roof, two twenty-four pounder guns were mounted on a central pivot, which enabled each gun to be rotated 360 degrees, so it could fire in any direction. A shot furnace allowed cannon balls to be heated to red-hot, the intention being that these would ignite the sails or rigging when fired on an enemy ship. The construction of Martello towers was discontinued after about 1850, when it was discovered they could not withstand the new generation of rifled artillery weapons.

Left: View of machicolated musketry position over doorway.
Top: View of rising tower wall.
Above: View of tower from west.

Tirkane Sweat House

County Derry

Map no. 33; GPS: N 54.865, W 6.711016; Irish Grid: C 82813 02680

The Irish sweat house, a cross between a Finnish sauna and a Turkish bath, was considered very effective in treating rheumatism and many other illnesses. Tirkane is a well-preserved, eighteenth century example, set in a magical secluded grove. Stone walls and a paved floor are surmounted by a roof made of lintelled flat stones. The structure is covered in turf leaving only a small air hole in the roof and a 40cm square doorway. The interior measures just 1m wide, 2.5m long and about 1.7m high. This small space was considered large enough for about four people. The sweat house was operated by lighting a large fire at the centre of its interior. The fire was continuously supplied with fuel for up to two days, until the whole structure was thoroughly heated. The newly swept floor was laid with rushes or bracken onto which water could be thrown to provide extra steam. The entrance was covered after the undressed patients had crawled in. They were then left to sweat it out and when they emerged a nearby plunge hole and stream could be used to cool off. Monsieur De Latocnaye recorded in his 1796, *A Frenchman's Walk Through Ireland*, that patients were kept in the sweat house for up to four or five hours and that they often emerged much thinner than when they went in. Most sweat houses went out of use by the end of the nineteenth century, however, one example in County Longford, regrettably demolished in 1975 to make way for a silage yard, was used in 1924 by a man who had been injured in a car accident. It seems that the doors of sweat houses were sometimes blocked up with the patient's clothes and a popular prank was to remove the clothes and run off with them.

Beltany Stone Circle

County Donegal

Map no. 34; GPS: N 54.850417, W 7.60467; Irish Grid: C 25442 00366

Beltany Stone Circle is situated about 1.5km south of Raphoe, on the summit of Tops Hill. It is 44m in diameter and originally contained about eighty stones of which sixty-four now remain. The stones range in height from 1.2m to 2.7m and are arranged around a low earth platform. A single stone about 2m high stands to the southeast of the circle. Various alignments have been suggested, the most persuasive being that aligning the high pillar at the southwest to the triangular stone decorated with cup marks at the east-northeast, points to Tullyrap hill about 8km away. This is where the sun rises on the first days of May, the ancient festival of Bealtaine, from which the circle derives its name. The site was disturbed during the first part of the twentieth century and when Oliver Davies, a prominent archaeologist, visited the site in the late 1930s, he reported that 'the platform had been recently and unscientifically excavated, and had been left in dreadful confusion'. A carved stone head reputably found close to the circle is now housed in the National Museum.

Above: Cup-marked stone is second stone from left.
Left: View of site from north.

COUNTY DONEGAL: BELTANY STONE CIRCLE   81

Cloncha Church and High Cross

County Donegal

Map no. 35; GPS: N 55.268701, W 7.174244; Irish Grid: C 52539 47172

Cloncha Church dates from the seventeenth century and was built on the site of an earlier monastery, founded by St Buodan. The lintel over the west door of the church was probably reused from this earlier structure. It has worn figure carvings and probably dates from the twelfth century. In the field to the west of the church a tenth- or eleventh-century high cross, repaired about 1980, stands almost 4m tall. It was carved from a single piece of stone and decorated with panels of geometric patterns and figure carving. On its east face a scene depicts the Miracle of the Loaves and Fishes. Further to the west is the head of a second cross and to the southwest a fallen standing stone. Within the church is an elaborate grave slab decorated with foliage, a sword, and a ball and caman (a hooked stick for playing the Scottish ball game shinty). Text is inscribed on the slab: 'FERGUS MAK ALAN DO RINI IN CLACH SA MAGNUS MEC ORRISTIN IA FO TRL SEO' which can be translated as 'Fergus Mac Allan made this stone and Magnus Mac Orristin lies under it'. Folklore tells that the slab originated from a churchyard on one of the Scottish islands and was brought to Ireland when a local fishing boat was blown to the island and required extra ballast to make the voyage home.

Left: Grave slab of Magnus Mac Orristin, decorated with foliage, a sword, and a ball and caman (for playing the Scottish game shinty).
Below: View of church interior looking east.
Bottom: View of site from south.

Doe Castle

County Donegal

Map no. 36; GPS: N 55.135163, W 7.863854; Irish Grid: C 08731 32003

Doe Castle was built on a peninsula on the edge of Sheephaven Bay by the Mac Sweeney family in the first part of sixteenth century. The four-storey tower house is enclosed by a high outer wall, with a moat cut into the rock on the landward side. A grave slab on the outside of the north face of the tower records the date 1544 and was probably carved for a member of the Mac Sweeney family. In 1642, Owen Roe O'Neill returned from Europe, landing at Doe Castle to lead the Irish Confederate forces as the northern commander of the Irish rebellion. In 1650, the castle was captured by Sir Charles Coote, Governor of Derry. Over the following years it changed hands a number of times and ended up in the ownership of the Harte family. It was inherited by General George Vaughan Harte in 1797, and on his return from fighting in India, he restored the castle, making it his family home. His initials GVH are displayed above the door of the eastern entrance. General Harte apparently returned from India with a Hindu soldier who acted as his personal bodyguard. This guard slept fully armed and still dressed in his oriental uniform on a rug outside the general's bedroom door. The general fell to his death down the stone steps leading to the banqueting room and his bodyguard died broken-hearted a few years later. The general's son, also called George Vaughan Harte, inherited the castle and, on his death in 1866, it was purchased by Mr Stewart of the neighbouring Ards estate. Doe Castle was bought by the OPW in 1932.

Top: View of castle from east within the courtyard. (Note letters 'CVH' in brick above the larger door.) **Above:** View inside outer wall from south.

Donegal Castle

County Donegal

Map no. 37; GPS: N 54.655054, W 8.110914; Irish Grid: G 92889 78551

Donegal Castle is situated in the centre of Donegal town at a bend of the River Eske. The first structure on the site was a simple tower house, built by the powerful O'Donnell clan in the late fifteenth or sixteenth century. In 1566, Sir Henry Sidney described the castle as 'one of the greatest that ever I saw in any Irishman's hands, and would appear in good keeping'. About 1600, Hugh Roe O'Donnell burnt the castle to prevent it being of use to the approaching English forces. He left to fight at the Battle of Kinsale and after suffering defeat, left Ireland in the Flight of the Earls. In 1623, the borough of Donegal, including the castle, was granted to Sir Basil Brooke, a captain in the English army. Brooke repaired and remodelled the tower house, adding mullioned windows and numerous gables. He then added a large three-story, Jacobean, gabled mansion house to the side of the tower. Sir Basil and his son, Sir Henry Brooke, both served as Governors of County Donegal. Henry sided with the Parliamentarians and lost the castle to the Royalist Earl of Clanricarde, but regained the castle just three days later. The Brooke family retained the castle for a few more generations but in the eighteenth century it was let fall into ruin. The castle eventually came into the ownership of the Earl of Arran, who maintained the ruin in good order. In 1898, the Earl donated the castle to the State. The tower house was superbly restored by the OPW in the 1990s with the mansion house left as a ruin.

Clockwise from top:
View of first floor room with bay window and fine chimney piece; Interior view of finely restored castle roof; View through mansion house doorway.

Grianán of Aileach Cashel and Hillfort

County Donegal

Map no. 38; GPS: N 55.023816, W 7.428052; Irish Grid: C 36629 19748

The Grianán of Aileach is built on the 244m-high hill of Grianán (or Greenan), about 10km northwest of Derry and overlooking Lough Foyle and Lough Swilly. It consists of three much-eroded concentric ramparts formed of earth and stone, with a stone ringfort or cashel at the centre. The ramparts were probably built in the Late Bronze Age or Iron Age. The outer rampart encloses an area of about 5.5 acres and the inner about 1 acre. The fort was probably built in the eighth century. It consists of a circular 5m-high stone wall, with a width of between 3.5m and 4.6m, enclosing an area 23.6m in diameter. The interior is accessed by a 4.6m-long lintelled passageway. Within the fort's walls are two passages which extend almost to the entrance passage; they are accessed by two small openings, one at the south and one at the northeast. The interior walls rise in three terraces, accessible by inset stairways. Grianán of Aileach was a seat of the northern Uí Néill, the rulers of Ulster. In 1101, it was attacked by Murtagh O'Brien, King of Munster. According to legend, O'Brien ordered its obliteration in revenge for the destruction of his royal seat at Kincora, County Clare. After attacking the fort, each of his soldiers took away a stone from its walls as they departed. Between 1874 and 1879, the fort was restored by Dr Walter Bernard. The restored sections include almost everything higher than 1m above ground.

Clockwise from top:
View over fort walls to
Lough Foyle; View of interior
steps to ramparts; View of
fort walls.

Newmills Corn and Flax Mills

County Donegal

Map no. 39; GPS: N 54.929139, W 7.808104; Irish Grid: C 12350 09075

Newmills corn and flax mills are located 5km west of Letterkenny, on the banks of the River Swilly. The first water mill on the site was recorded in 1683. The site continued to be developed and by the early 1800s, Joesph Hunter was operating both a corn and flax mill. In 1861, the mills were sold to John Devine. John's son, William sold the enterprise in 1892 to Patrick Gallagher, it then consisted of the mills, a residence, a public house and grocery. At this time the corn mill was disused and its buildings in a poor state of repair. Gallagher made extensive improvements including the fitting of a huge new waterwheel, which is still present today. During the Second World War, Gallagher took advantage of British Government grants offered to increase production of flax to supply linen required in the war effort. He demolished the old flax mill and built the flax mill which stands on the site to this day. The mills continued in operation until the death of Patrick Gallagher's son, also called Patrick in 1980. An inventory of industrial archaeology recognised that the mill complex is an exceptional surviving example and in 1986 it was purchased by the State for preservation as a National Monument. Over the following years the waterwheels were restored and the machinery of both mills repaired. The dam across the River Swilly, the mill pond and the millrace were all rebuilt. Today the mills are operated by the OPW as a free entry museum and visitor centre.

Clockwise from top:
View of corn mill feed hoppers;
View of flax mill scutching machinery;
View of corn mill waterwheel.

Ballycopeland Windmill

County Down

Map no. 40; GPS: N 54.607832, W 5.556228; Irish Grid: J 57947 76035

County Down is one of the best grain growing areas in Ireland and in the 1890s there were eighty-nine corn mills recorded as working in the county. By the 1960s virtually all these mills had ceased operation owing to more profitable large scale milling at ship ports. Ballycopeland mill was built in the 1780s and was operated by the McGilton family from 1845 to 1915. Samuel McGilton, who was the last miller, offered it to the State in 1937, after more than twenty years of disuse. Structural repairs were then carried out to the cap and sails and further major work was carried out in the 1950s. In 1978, the mill was fully restored to working condition and it is now the only complete and operational windmill in Ireland. Its tower is built of local stone, with the walls about 60cm thick. The mill stands about 10m high and has a base diameter of nearly 7m. The cap of the mill can be turned by an automatic fantail, ensuring the sails always face directly into the wind. Power is transmitted from the sails through the windshaft, brake wheel and wallower, to a vertical driveshaft which runs to the floors below. This vertical shaft was made from a reclaimed ship's mast, as indicated by rope friction marks in the wood. Above ground level are another three floors: the drive floor, stone floor and hopper floor. Sacks were raised by a hoist to the hopper floor, where the grain was fed down to the three pairs of mill stones. Chutes from the mill stones directed the processed grain to fill sacks on the ground floor. The mill produced oatmeal and wheatmeal for human consumption and processed oats, maize, kibbled grain, peas and beans for animal feed. Next to the windmill can be found the restored miller's house and kiln-house, which houses a visitor centre during the tourist season.

Left: View of automatic fantail mechanism.
Right: View of windmill from southeast.
Below: View of miller's house and kiln-house.

Ballynahatty Giant's Ring

County Down

Map no.41; GPS: N 54.540455, W 5.950427; Irish Grid: J 32699 67722

The Giant's Ring, in the townland of Ballynahatty, lies about 6km from the centre of Belfast. It consists of a 4m-high grass bank, surrounding a circular enclosure measuring about 200m across. The remains of a Neolithic passage grave are located near the centre of the ring. The bank was probably built at the end of the Neolithic or the beginning of the Bronze Age, enclosing the earlier passage grave. It was built from material excavated from within the enclosure, a task which, it is estimated, would have required at least 70,000 hours of labour. In November 1855, Mr Bodel, who farmed the land just northwest of the ring, discovered a circular stone tomb whilst digging potatoes. After removing the covering slab two boys who were in the field at the time descended into the tomb. They discovered a chamber about 2m long and 1m wide which contained three human skulls and an urn filled with cremated bones. Excavation over the following week revealed four more urns and more cremated bone. The Giant's Ring was investigated several times over the following years, but nothing very remarkable was discovered until 1989, when aerial photography showed that the ring was part of a large complex (33 hectares) of ceremonial and burial monuments including ring-ditches. One of the investigated features, about 100m to the northwest, was

a large, oval enclosure of paired timbers dated by radiocarbon dating to the Late Neolithic. A smaller, double-ring timber circle was found within the larger circle and a square post feature may have been a platform for the exposure of corpses. Though we can only make an educated guess at the purpose of the Giant's Ring, it is likely that it was used for ritual during funerary ceremonies.

View of passage grave near the centre of the ring with bank in background.

Grey Abbey

County Down

Map no. 42; GPS: N 54.53702, W 5.555048; Irish Grid: J 58297 68158

Grey Abbey was founded on 25 August 1193, by the beautiful Princess Affreca, daughter of the King of the Isle of Man, and wife of Sir John de Courcy. The story goes that on her voyage to Ireland, the princess's ship became caught in a terrible storm and just as the ship's crew thought they were about to perish, Affreca pleaded for help from Heaven. Apparently a beam of light shone from the sky and as the storm melted away, she promised to build a church and monastery for the honour of God. Cistercian monks were brought over from the Abbey of Holm Cultram in Cumberland and the grey colour of their robes gave the name to the new abbey and the village that grew up around it. Grey Abbey and Inch Abbey were the first fully Gothic-styled buildings in Ireland with almost every arch and doorway pointed, rather than the earlier round-headed arches of the Romanesque period. The ruins today comprise the church and some remnants of the vestry, chapter house, day room, warming house and refectory. Nothing remains of the cloister or the west range. Grey Abbey was dissolved in 1541. The buildings

were burnt by Sir Brian O'Neill in 1572, to stop them being fortified and used by the English. In 1607, the lands were granted to Sir Hugh Montgomery. The first Viscount Montgomery re-roofed the nave of the church and it was used as a parish church from 1626 until a new church was built just to the north in 1778. In 1908, Major W. E. Montgomery transferred the abbey into State care. In the early twentieth century, buttresses were added to prevent collapse of the southern nave wall which was cracked and severely bowed.

Opposite page: View through west doorway to east lancet windows (left); View of church nave from crossing tower (right).
Top: View of site from south.
Left: View of remains of refectory.

Inch Abbey

County Down

Map no.43; GPS: N 54.336595, W 5.731001; Irish Grid: J 47630 45471

Inch Abbey derives its name from the Irish word *Inis* or Island, for it was once surrounded by the nearby River Quoile, which now flows only on its southern side. An early monastic settlement was in existence on the island by the year 800. It was plundered by Vikings in 1001, when many of its occupants were taken prisoner. In 1177, during his invasion of Ulster, Sir John de Courcy attacked and demolished Erynagh Abbey, located about 5km away. Even though Erynagh had been fortified against him and used as a garrison, de Courcy felt the need to make compensation for his sacrilegious act and brought Cistercian monks over from Furness Abbey in Lancashire and founded the Abbey of Inch. St Evodius, the first abbot of Erynagh appears to have prophesised this event as on his deathbed he requested that his body be interred on *Inis*, declaring that his own abbey would be destroyed and later rebuilt on that island. Inch Abbey had a strong Anglo-Norman influence and in 1380, Irishmen were refused entry into the monastery. This appears to have put the monastic population into decline and a fire in 1404 gave the opportunity for a drastic reduction in the size of the church. The transepts were walled off and the earlier vast

nave was divided by a new west wall and doorway. The dissolution of the monasteries brought about the final end of monastic life at Inch. In 1542, the monastery was formally dissolved. It passed through several owners before becoming the property of the Perceval Maxwell family. The Perceval Maxwells carried out some repairs before putting the abbey into State care in 1910. Subsequently much more preservation and restoration of the abbey buildings was carried out.

Clockwise from above:
View of abbey remains from southwest; Remains of spiral stairway in north tower; View of northern transept and open twin chapels with blocked transept arch.

Struell Wells

County Down

Map no. 44; GPS: N 54.324095, W 5.677443; Irish Grid: J 51158 44193

The wells derive their name from the Irish word *tsruthail* or stream. The stream, which was said to have been blessed by St Patrick, is diverted through a system of medieval culverts to four different holy wells. The Drinking Well, a beehive-shaped stone building, is where legend tells of St Patrick spending the night standing in the water, stark naked, singing psalms and spiritual songs. The Eye Well, a small rectangular structure at the centre of the site, was traditionally used for curing the blind. To the southeast are the Men's and Women's Bathing Wells. The Men's Well has a room for undressing with a doorway leading to a dark chamber, holding a deep rectangular bathing tank. In the Women's Well, a water outlet in the wall was used rather like a shower. In earlier times the baths were mixed sex and whilst the shower was free, payment was required to access the more comfortable bathing tank. Struell was a popular pilgrimage destination, particularly around midsummer, when the miraculous power of the water was said to reach maximum potency. Around this time, more than 1,000 people would gather daily to undergo penance and use the holy wells. A further huge crowd would gather in the hope of witnessing a miracle. Accommodation was provided by many tents that, according to records, offered whiskey and every kind of entertainment. It was believed that whilst on sacred ground no new sins could be committed and hence riotous orgies were not uncommon. The scandalous activities at Struell did not go down well with the Catholic Church and the priests' use of the wells was discontinued in about 1804. Archbishop William Crolly eventually had the field in front of the wells ploughed up to discourage access and the pilgrimages had ceased by about 1870.

Left: View of the Eye Well.
Right: View of Men's Well side chamber, possibly used as the women's changing room.
Opposite page: View of site from northwest (top); View of the drinking well (bottom).

Ballyedmonduff Wedge Tomb

County Dublin

Map no. 45; GPS: N 53.229044, W 6.226373; Irish Grid: O 18494 21289

This early Bronze Age wedge tomb is located close to the edge of a pine forest on the lower slopes of Two Rock Mountain at a height of about 340m. It was first discovered by Alderman Blacker *c.* 1830. At this time the forest had not been planted and the tomb was completely covered by an oval mound of earth. By 1837, at the time of the first Ordnance Survey (OS), some of the mound had been removed, revealing the chamber structure. The surveyor described the tomb as one of the most perfectly preserved to be found in Ireland. It is shown on the first OS map as 'Giants Grave'. In March 1945, the tomb was excavated by an archaeological team from University College Dublin. The remains of the surrounding mound measured 17m long by 12m wide and reached a height of about 2m. Unfortunately in the years since the OS survey, many of the stones have been removed and others damaged by stonecutters. The main chamber has been largely destroyed with the entire north side being completely removed. The excavations revealed that the structure of the tomb comprised a gallery, oriented approximately east–west, which was divided into three chambers. Finds included many fragments of pottery, a number of flints, a polished hammer stone and a few fragments of cremated bone. The edge of the cairn is defined by a horseshoe-shaped kerb with the façade and entrance to the tomb at the western end. A stone on the southern side is decorated with seven cup marks.

View of tomb chambers from west.

Casino at Marino

County Dublin

Map no. 46; GPS: N 53.371354, W 6.227006; Irish Grid: O 18058 37125

In 1754, James Caulfied, Earl of Charlemont, was given a house named The Lodge, by his stepfather, Thomas Adderley. He renamed it Marino Lodge and began to enlarge and improve it. In 1757 he employed the architect William Chambers to design a garden temple or *casino* (Italian for small country house). Its construction became a labour of love, taking nearly twenty years, at a cost of over £30,000 (about €5 million today). In plan it forms the shape of a Greek cross. It is encircled by twelve columns and sits on a square podium, surrounded by a deep light well. From the outside it appears compact, giving the illusion of containing just one room. The podium, however, contains eight servant's rooms, the *piano nobile* (Italian for the principle floor) contains five rooms including the Saloon, Vestibule and Zodiac Room and there are another three rooms, including Lord Charlemont's bedchamber in the attic. Many tricks were used to preserve the simplicity of design: four of the columns that surround the building are hollow, to drain rainwater from the roof, and the urns on the roof are disguised chimneys. The Earl opened his Marino parkland to the public, perhaps a mistake as the lead was soon stolen from its roof. After his death in 1799, Marino passed to his widow, and then to his son, Francis, who had little interest in the estate. The third Earl gave up on Marino altogether and sold it to the Christian Brothers in 1876. Marino Lodge was set on fire during the Troubles of 1921 and then demolished to make way for the Marino housing estate. In 1972, the Casino was vested into State care. After a restoration project that lasted ten years, the Casino is one of the finest eighteenth-century garden pavilions in Europe.

Top: Lord Charlemont's bedchamber. **Bottom:** View of vestibule.

Kilmainham Gaol

County Dublin

Map no. 47; GPS: N 53.341642, W 6.308877; Irish Grid: O 12688 33686

In 1784, the old Dublin County Jail comprised three underground dungeons which held sixty-four prisoners. There were regular escapes and a report concluded 'there was not so weak or ill conceived a jail as the County Dublin one'. In 1786, a Bill was passed through Parliament enabling a new County Gaol to be constructed and Sir John Traile was appointed architect. The jail was finally completed in 1796 at a cost of £22,000. It was said to be superior to any prison in Europe. The main building comprised two quadrangles, enclosing two courtyards. There were fifty-two cells, each measuring about 3m by 2m. Initially there were twenty-six prisoners, including eight accused of high treason, five debtors, an unnamed dentist who had been incarcerated for breaking the tooth of a magistrate, and the jailer of St Sepulchre Jail who was charged with extortion of fees. The first jail keeper, Robert Ware, was suspended following a breakout of three men in 1797. His successor was also suspended following an escape in 1807. In 1858, the prison was extended with the addition of the west wing. Modelled on Pentonville Prison in London, it is a vast three-storey space surrounded by catwalks onto which the cells open. Following the failure of the 1916 Easter Rising, Padraig Pearse and thirteen other rebel leaders were executed by firing squad in

the prison stonebreaker's yard. During the Civil War many executions of anti-treaty Republican prisoners were also carried out at the jail. It was decommissioned as a prison by the Irish Free State government in 1924 and left to deteriorate until it was leased to a voluntary restoration committee in 1960. In 1986, it was transferred into the care of the OPW and is now a very popular tourist destination.

Clockwise from top left:
View of cell door; View of prison corridor with cells to right; View of upper level corridor with cells to right; Stonebreaker's yard: the cross marks where anti-treaty Republican prisoners were executed.

Rathfarnham Castle

County Dublin

Map no. 48; GPS: N 53.29812, W 6.283665; Irish Grid: O 14483 28883

Rathfarnham Castle was built in 1583 by Adam Loftus, Protestant Archbishop of Dublin and Lord Chancellor. The structure was rectangular in plan with projecting towers at each corner, and originally strongly fortified, similar in appearance to Kanturk Castle, County Cork (p. 68). It resisted attacks by the Wicklow clans in 1600 and a siege during the 1641 Rebellion. Sir Adam Loftus lost possession of the castle in the Irish Confederate Wars and it changed hands several times, being garrisoned by both Parliamentary and Royalist troops. After the Restoration of Charles II, it was returned to the Loftus family, but later passed to the Marquess of Wharton with his marriage to the heiress, Lucy Loftus. In 1723, the estate was sold to William Conolly, Speaker of the House of Commons, for £62,000. It passed through a few more hands, before returning to the Loftus family in 1767, when purchased by Nicholas Loftus. Henry Loftus, created Earl of Ely in 1771, inherited the castle and extensively remodelled it. A new entrance gate was added in the form of a Roman triumphal arch. The battlements were replaced with ornamented stone coping, the mullioned windows enlarged and modernised, and the interior magnificently redecorated. The

Loftus family left Rathfarnham for the last time in 1812. For the next forty years the estate was used as a dairy farm, before being purchased by Francis Blackbourne, Lord Chancellor. In 1912, the estate was acquired by property developers and the land divided. The castle was sold to the Society of Jesus, who used it as an ecclesiastical college. In 1985, the castle was again acquired by property developers and, after fears of demolition, it was purchased by the Irish State in 1987. The castle now houses the Berkeley Costumes and Toy Collection.

Left: View through pedimented hall doorway.
Top: View of castle gallery.
Above: View with pieces from the Berkeley Costumes and Toy Collection, now housed at the castle.

Tibradden Cairn

County Dublin

Map no. 49; GPS: N 53.238622, W 6.280339; Irish Grid: O 14864 22267

Tibradden Cairn is located close to the summit of Tibradden Mountain, at a height of 460m. The cairn measures approximately 12m in diameter. A 5m-long passage leads from the northeast into a circular chamber 3m in diameter, with the surrounding cairn walls reaching a height of about 1m. On the floor of the chamber is a stone inscribed with two spiral patterns. The previously undisturbed cairn was opened in June 1849 by Marcus Harty and the gamekeeper of the mountain, Michael Mahon. The two men removed stones from the top of the cairn until they revealed a rectangular, stone-lined cist, approximately 1m long by 0.5m wide and 0.3m deep. A burial urn, measuring 10cm high, with a diameter of 14cm, was found inside the cist. It contained charcoal and cremated remains and was placed in the Royal Irish Academy museum in 1859. A second urn was found outside the central chamber, bottom up, against the cairn stones. It was in a bad state of decay and was not preserved. Investigation and conservation work carried out by the OPW in 1956 confirmed the suspicion that the chamber and passage were not part of the original structure and had been inserted *c.* 1850 to give access to the cist and transform the cairn into a kind of folly. The stone with inscribed spirals is also probably of mid-nineteenth-century provenance.

Stone with inscribed spirals: probably a nineteenth-century addition.

Devenish Island Monastic Site

County Fermanagh

Map no. 50; GPS: N 54.368709; W 7.654982; Irish Grid: H 22474 46725

Devenish derives its name from the Irish *Daimh Inis* or Ox Island and is one of the many islands on Lower Lough Erne. St Molaise founded a monastic settlement here in the sixth century. The settlement thrived but suffered Viking attacks in 836 and 923. The fine round tower, with decorated cornice and, close to it, St Molaise's House, both date from the twelfth century and are the earliest surviving remains on the island. The tower was repaired in 1835 after a tree had started to grow from under its conical cap. St Molaise's House stood in fine condition into the eighteenth century, until the Bishop of Clogher apparently ordered its cut stone to be removed and used in the church of Enniskillen. After this the island tended to serve as a quarry for locals who needed building material. *Teampull Mór*, the lower church, dates from the early thirteenth century and was later extended to the east. St Mary's Augustinian Priory, on the hilltop, dates from the fifteenth century. It comprised a church, tower, sacristy, chapter house, refectory and a small cloister. The priory also suffered from architectural salvage. A finely carved window, which stood over the high altar, was removed to the Church of St Molaise in Monea,

County Fermanagh, and an engraved stone which recorded that Matthew O'Doogan built the priory in 1449 for Bartholomew O'Flannagan, was removed by Captain Fitzmairs and inserted above the doorway of a toilet block in Enniskillen barracks. Protests and legal threats, however, forced the captain to return this stone to the priory. The dissolution of the monasteries brought an end to the Augustinians' priory and parish worship moved off the island in 1630. The graveyards on Devenish continued to be used until disaster struck in 1824, when a boat carrying mourners to the island overturned and twenty-six people drowned.

Clockwise from top: View of site from southwest. (Note unusual fifteenth-century cross.); View through west door into St Mary's Augustinian Priory; View of *Teampull Mór* from the north.

Monea Castle

County Fermanagh

Map no. 51; GPS: N 54.393527, W 7.74785; Irish Grid: H 16428 49462

Sir Robert Hamilton received a grant of 1,500 'profitable acres' of land as part of the Plantation of Ulster. In 1618, his son, Malcolm, completed the Scottish-style Monea Castle and in 1622 added the defensive bawn. The castle is about 17m long and 6m wide. It stood three storeys high with tall attics and a thatched roof. At the west end, a pair of massive semi-cylindrical towers provided a defensive position over the castle entrance. The gloomy vaulted basement was lit only by musket loops and contained the kitchens and wine cellar. The principal rooms were on the first floor and were illuminated by large windows with seats in the embrasures. On the second floor were bedchambers and latrines with a chute which emptied on the outside of the east wall. Though in places the bawn wall is almost reduced to its foundations, it once stood about 4m high and had flanking towers on the opposing corners to the castle. The remains of the tower at the northwest has compartments in the interior walls, indicating that it was later used as a dovecote. In 1641, the castle was attacked by an army of men under the rebel leader Rory Maguire. According to an eyewitness eight people inside the castle were killed but Maguire's men failed to capture the castle. It remained home to the Hamilton family and in 1688 was occupied by Gustavus Hamilton, Governor of Enniskillen. The castle was finally abandoned after a fire in about 1750. Its spiral stairs were deliberately broken at the start of the nineteenth century by Owen Keenan to stop his family of young boys enjoying their dangerous pastime of climbing to the most perilous parts of the crumbling walls. Monea Castle was taken into State care in 1954.

Left: View of castle from southwest. (Note the Scottish inspired towers.)
Top: View of castle interior.
Above: View upwards inside south tower.

Tully Castle

County Fermanagh

Map no. 52; GPS: N 54.458053, W 7.805539; Irish Grid: H 12660 56633

In 1610, as part of the Plantation of Ulster, Sir John Hume from Berwickshire in Scotland was granted 2,000 'profitable acres' of land at Tully on the west shore of Lower Lough Erne. He set about building a castle and bawn, which were completed by the year 1613. The bawn measured about 30m square, with walls over 4m high. At each corner, the walls were surmounted by a defensive flanking tower. Hume built a typical early-seventeenth-century, Scottish-style castle inside the bawn. It stood three storeys high and measured about 14m long by 7m wide. Hume also built a village close by which housed twenty-four families. The life of the castle was tragically short. On Christmas Eve 1641, it was attacked by a force of 800 men under the rebel leader Rory Maguire. Lady Hume surrendered on condition that she, her family and about eighty other settlers who had sought refuge in the castle, were given safe passage to Monea Castle or Enniskillen. On their surrender, the rebels took the castle's occupants prisoner. All except Lady Hume were stripped of their clothes. The men's hands and feet were bound and they were held overnight in the castle courtyard. The next day, Christmas Day, Lady Hume and her immediate family were transferred into a nearby barn. Maguire's men then massacred all the remaining prisoners: sixteen men and sixty-nine women and children. Tully Castle was then pillaged and burnt and left in the ruinous condition that it remains in to this day.

Clockwise from top: View of vaulted castle basement; View of gardens through castle window; Interior view of south wall of castle.

Derryhivenny Castle

County Galway

Map no. 53; GPS: N 53.127088, W 8.19226; Irish Grid: M 87179 08490

The O'Madden family was established on the lands around Derryhivenny from about the year 950. On 5 February 1639, the then head of the family, John O'Madden, died, leaving his estate to his son, Daniel, who a few years later built Derryhivenny Castle. The tower house was located in an L-shaped bawn which had circular towers on two corners. A single-storey rectangular building, probably the main hall, was built against the side of the eastern curtain wall. An inscription found on one of the corbels of the bartizan at the northeastern angle of the tower records the date of construction as 1643, 'D : OM ME : FIERI : FECIT : 1643', making Derryhivenny one of the last true tower houses erected in Ireland. Little is known of its subsequent history, although from the well-preserved condition of the structure it was probably peaceful. The stonework of the tower is in very good condition, except for the upper sections of the parapet walls. Externally the tower measures about 12m by 10m at the base and rises to a height of over 16m, with the Jacobean chimney stacks extending a further 5m. The tower is entered through a pointed doorway in the east wall, which leads into an entrance lobby. From here there is a small guardroom to

the right and, directly ahead, a loophole or spy hole. A doorway to the left leads to the inner lobby and a short, straight flight of six steps. These steps led to a spiral staircase which accessed the upper floors and roofs. All the main floors of the tower were built of timber and, with the ravages of time, these have long since disappeared, leaving the structure today as almost an empty shell.

Left: View of castle from southwest showing one of the round flanking turrets. **Top:** View upwards of tower house interior, showing numerous fireplaces. **Above:** View of internal doorway. (Note decorated dressed stones.)

Glinsk Castle

County Galway

Map no. 54; GPS: N 53.65204, W 8.431857; Irish Grid: M 71493 66985

Glinsk Castle, a semi-fortified house, is said to have been built by Sir Ulick Burke about 1630, shortly after he had been created a baronet of Ireland. The castle is three storeys high, over a raised basement, plus attic and is rectangular in plan with a recessed bay in the centre of the south side. There are two entrances, one on the north side, which is at ground level and led into the basement, and a second on the south side, inside the recessed bay, at first-floor level. The ground-level entrance is protected from above by a defensive machicolation, which allowed boiling water, oil or other projectiles to be thrown down on unwelcome visitors. There are similar machicolations on the southwest and southeast corners of the castle. All the windows at ground level are fitted with iron bars and are fashioned in the style of gun loops, opening at a wide angle on the interior, but with a narrow external opening. The upper floors have finely carved mullioned windows. One of the outstanding features of the castle is the elegant Jacobean chimney stacks, amongst the best examples of their kind in Ireland. The castle was destroyed by fire at an unrecorded date, though supposedly early in its history. Glinsk House was later built on a site just to the north of the castle, though by the first part of the nineteenth century this house was in a decrepit state and the Burke family fortune in decline. In 1853, the Glinsk estate, which comprised 3,361 acres, was sold to a Scottish timber merchant. By the first part of the twentieth century Glinsk House had been demolished without leaving any trace. Glinsk Castle is now under the guardianship of the OPW, and survives as a well-preserved shell.

View of house interior with Jacobean-style
chimney stacks at top.

Portumna Castle

County Galway

Map no. 55; GPS: N 53.086634, W 8.220745; Irish Grid: M 85258 03993

Portumna Castle, a semi-fortified house, was built about 1618, by Richard Burke, the fourth Earl of Clanricarde, and his wife, Frances Walsingham, Countess of Essex. The cost of its construction was £10,000, in those days a very considerable sum. The house is three storeys high over a basement, plus attic and is rectangular in shape with flankers at each corner. The internal structure comprised two similar sets of rooms, one on the north side and one on the south, joined longitudinally by a central hallway. The rooms were arranged so that the family could live on the south side of the house, whilst the north side formed an apartment which could be given over to important visitors. The house was approached from the town by a tree-lined avenue that led through a series of gateways, the last being the Tuscan gate which is placed in a courtyard aligned centrally with the main door. A second avenue led to the east of the house, which gave access to a service courtyard containing a brew house, wash house, stables and other outbuildings and leading to a servants' entrance into the main house. In 1826, an accidental fire left the house a burnt-out wreck. The family first converted the stables for residential use, before building a new house about 1km to the southwest. This new house was also destroyed by fire, though this time deliberately, during the Troubles of 1922. Portumna Castle and its demesne were sold to the Irish State in 1948 and subsequently passed into the care of the OPW. A conservation programme started in the 1960s and the house was re-roofed during the 1990s, after which an extensive research and restoration project commenced. An exhibition detailing the history of the house, its occupants and its restoration is on display in the main hall.

Above: View of house gardens from front door.
Left: Interior view of main hall.

Ross Errilly Friary

County Galway

Map no. 56; GPS: N 53.478903, W 9.131913; Irish Grid: M 24898 48225

The founding date for Ross Errilly Friary is disputed, with dates in the fourteenth and fifteenth centuries being suggested. It is, however, recorded as becoming part of the Observant Franciscan order in 1470. An inquiry in the middle of the sixteenth century records the friary complex as: 'a church, a cloister, a hall, dormitories, chambers, kitchen, and cellars; a cemetery, three small gardens, and a mill, which for want of water, could work only in winter.' An unusual feature is the second courtyard which housed the domestic buildings such as the refectory and kitchen. Most of the buildings can still be identified today, including the kitchen at the northwest corner, which is equipped with an oven and a water tank for holding live fish caught from the nearby Black River. The Franciscans strongly opposed Henry VIII's dissolution of the monasteries and in 1538, 200 friars were imprisoned. A royal patent granted the lands to Richard Burke, the second Earl of Clanricarde. The Earl, however, quietly returned it to the friars. In 1584, the friary was again confiscated and plundered but the Earl purchased it two years later, and again returned it to the friars. A similar pattern of events occurred in 1600 and 1612, with the friars again returning a few years later. Cromwellian forces reached the friary in 1656. The grounds were ransacked, crosses and other religious icons were destroyed and tombs looted. The 140 friars had received prior warning and fled unharmed some hours before. They returned a few years later and inhabited the friary until the Popery Act of 1698 made them fugitives. They abandoned the friary and secretly occupied a small island one mile downstream, where the local community supplied them with food and clothing via a wooden drawbridge. By 1801 only three friars remained and in 1832 they had disappeared altogether. Surprisingly, despite its many years of strife, the friary is amongst the best preserved medieval monastic sites in Ireland.

Above: View of cloister arcading.
Left: View to crossing tower from second courtyard.

Cahergal Cashel

County Kerry

Map no. 57; GPS: N 51.955983, W 10.257744; Irish Grid: V 44844 80559

On the summit of a small hillock, the stone fort at Cahergal measures over 20m in diameter, with the massive circular drystone wall about 2m high and 3m thick. The inner face of the wall is lined with a series of flights of steps, rising diagonally to narrow terraces. It was reconstructed by the OPW in the 1990s. At the centre of the fort are the remains of a *clochán*, or circular drystone hut, with a diameter of about 7m. This hut was once covered by a corbelled stone roof. As far as is known the stones fell in the late eighteenth century and were later used to build a shed for lambs within the hut's walls. Excavation of the *clochán* revealed a central hearth-pit which contained a large amount of ash, seemingly built up over many years. It is difficult to put a date on the fort's construction, though it is likely that a relatively prosperous family lived here about 1,000 years ago.

Gallarus Oratory

County Kerry

Map no. 58; GPS: N 52.172728, W 10.349368; Irish Grid: Q 39326 04871

Gallarus Oratory is the best known and best preserved of the Irish boat-shaped oratories, so called because their sloping curved walls form the shape of an upturned boat. The base of the structure is rectangular, measuring about 7m long by 5m wide. The walls, built from local red sandstone, are more than 1m thick and rise to a height of about 5m. The stonework is laid with a tilt towards the exterior, ensuring the driving west Kerry rain never entered the interior. The structure remains perfect to this day, never having required rebuilding or restoration. The oratory is entered through a 2m-high inclined square-headed doorway at the western end. Two projecting stones, with holes, indicate where the door once hung. At the eastern end there is a small round-headed window. There has been some debate regarding Gallarus's date of construction. One theory suggests it is an early Christian structure dating from the middle of the eighth century, making it one of the oldest stone churches in Ireland. More recent thinking places its period of construction in the twelfth century. Folklore relates that towards the end of the eighteenth century a boy climbed up the roof and stole a number of stones. As he dropped back down to the ground his body began to swell up until he reached almost the size of the oratory. It was left to the boy's mother to replace the stones quickly, whereupon he began to return to his normal size.

Kilmalkedar Church

County Kerry

Map no. 59; GPS: N 52.184905, W 10.336847; Irish Grid: Q 40227 06198

A monastic settlement was founded here by St Maolcethair (Malkedar), grandson of the King of Ulster, in the first part of the seventh century. The location was chosen probably due to its proximity to Mount Brandon, a pre-Christian religious symbol, which has a pilgrimage route leading to its summit. The Kilmalkedar settlement spread over a wide area and today its remains, which range in date from the early Christian period through to the fifteenth century, include the church, St Brendan's House, holy wells, an Ogham stone, bullaun stones, an oratory, a sundial and several cross-inscribed slabs. Kilmalkedar Church is twelfth-century Romanesque. The nave, which has *antae,* was built first, with the chancel added *c.* 1200, replacing the original altar recess. The church entrance, at the west end, is by a fine Romanesque doorway, with a carved human head on the exterior side and a bull or other beast on the interior. The roof was originally formed of corbelled stones, sections of which still remain in both the nave and chancel. The blind colonnade walls in the nave were perhaps influenced by Cormac's Chapel at Cashel. Standing next to the chancel arch is the 1.2m-high alphabet stone, with, on its west side, an inscription

of the Latin alphabet. Close to the path leading to the church is an early sundial, a large stone cross, and a holed Ogham stone, on which the inscription translates as 'Mael Inbir son of Brocán'. When the cross was excavated, it was found to extend a further 1.8m underground. Further to the north is the two-storey medieval building known as St Brendan's House. To the northwest, on the edge of a field, is St Brendan's Oratory, a boat-shaped oratory very similar to Gallarus, though with its roof collapsed.

Left: View of early sundial. **Top:** View of Romanesque chancel arch with alphabet stone at left. **Above:** View of site from west with ogham stone in foreground.

Muckross Friary

County Kerry

Map no. 60 ; GPS: N 52.026112, W 9.494816; Irish Grid: V 97448 87008

Muckross Friary was founded for the Observantine Franciscans by Donal MacCarthy Mór in 1448. Legend relates that Donal had a vision instructing the construction of the monastery at *Carraig-an-chiuil*, or The Rock of the Music. His men searched for such a place but did not find anywhere of that name. Returning home, they heard a sweet melody emerging from the rocky eastern pass, near the shore of Lough Leane and thus the site of the monastery was chosen. The chancel of the church is the earliest part of the well-preserved friary complex, with the remainder built in continuous stages until completed in about 1475. The south transept is a slightly later addition, built about 1500. The square cloister, attached to the north side of the nave, is very well preserved and the large yew tree within is at least 350 years old. Following the dissolution of the monasteries, the friary was officially suppressed in 1541. The friars, however, remained in residence until they were attacked in 1589. Father O'Muirthile and several of his companions, who had rowed across the lake to hide their sacred vessels, were captured and put to death by English soldiers. The friars returned in 1612 and started to restore the friary, work which lasted until 1626. Just three years later they were again forced to leave, but they returned some years later. They were finally driven out by Cromwell's Soldiers of Fortune in 1652 and outlawed by the Penal Laws of 1698. The friary was eventually transferred into state ownership and the OPW cleared the ruin of overgrowth and carried out extensive restoration work in the 1930s. In 1864, a stone was taken from the friary ruins and carried into Killarney town, where it was used as the foundation stone for a new friary church for the Franciscans. The Franciscans still operate from this church today.

Clockwise from top left: View from nave into south transept; View from nave to crossing tower; View of west door of church; View of vaulted ground-floor room in north range.

Ross Castle

County Kerry

Map no. 61; GPS: N 52.041273, W 9.531734; Irish Grid: V 94949 88748

Ross Castle was built in the late fifteenth century by one of the O'Donoghue Mór chieftains, hereditary rulers of the area and descendants of the ancient kings of Munster. The original structure comprised a tower house surrounded by a square bawn, with circular flanking towers. Following the Desmond Rebellions, Rory O'Donoghue Mór forfeited his lands and Ross was acquired by the MacCarthy Mórs, who sold it to the Browne family in about 1588. In 1652, Cormac MacCarthy Mór, Lord Muskerry, was the guardian of his young nephew Sir Valentine Browne. Lord Muskerry was in command of the Munster forces of the Confederate Catholics and retreated to his nephew's castle after the Battle of Knockiclashy, with a force of about 1,500 men. General Ludlow, in command of the Parliamentary forces, followed in hot pursuit with 1,500 men on foot and a further 700 on horse. Not seeing any way to capture the castle, Ludlow took account of a legend that foretold the castle would fall to a warship that approached from the lake. He arranged for a number of ships to be prepared by carpenters in Kinsale, such that they could be transported overland and quickly assembled at Ross. The boats arrived on 18 June 1652 and four days

later Lord Muskerry signed his surrender. Sir Valentine Browne managed to retain the castle as he was then just twelve years old. In about 1688, he added a large mansion house to the south side of the castle but as he supported the Jacobite cause, he forfeited the estate in 1690. The castle was then used as a military barracks. The Brownes recovered their lands around 1720 and built the more comfortable Kenmare House in Killarney town. Ross Castle was eventually abandoned and fell into total disrepair. The OPW restored it in the 1980s.

Left: View of tower-house entrance. **Top:** View of castle from west. **Above:** Interior view of upper room.

Skellig Michael Monastery

County Kerry

Map no. 62; GPS: N 51.771239, W 10.539279; Irish Grid: V 24776 60646

Located about 2km west of the Kerry coastline, on the western edge of Europe, is the pyramidal rocky island of Skellig Michael. Close to its summit at a height of about 200m are the remains of a monastic settlement, thought to have been founded by St Fionan in the sixth century. The first record of the settlement occurs in the Annals of Ulster, when in AD 823 Eitgal of Skellig was carried off by Vikings and died of hunger and thirst. In 838, the Vikings again returned and laid waste to the island's churches. The Annals also record the deaths of Blathmhac of Skellig in 950 and Aedh of Skellig in 1040. The original landing place was a little cove deep in the recess of a cave, which could only be approached in calm seas. Today a large pier allows far easier access. The path which ascends the island starts at a gentle angle, but then changes to long flights of very steep, crude steps. Near the summit a series of terraces holds the remains of the monastery, including six beehive huts, two rectangular oratories, St Michael's Church and the Monks' Garden. The extreme remoteness and a general climatic deterioration prompted the community to relocate to the mainland in the latter part of the twelfth century, where they had founded a second monastery at Ballinskelligs. This was suppressed around 1540, after the dissolution of the monasteries. Although Skellig Michael was no longer permanently occupied, it continued to be a place of pilgrimage. Around 1826, the island was sold to the Commissioners of Irish Lights, who built two lighthouses on the Atlantic side of the island. In 1880, the island was taken into State care and in 1996 it was listed as an UNESCO World Heritage Site.

Top: View of monks' graveyard. **Above:** View of Skellig Michael from northeast.

Conolly's Folly

County Kildare

Map no. 63; GPS: N 53.369068, W 6.561928; Irish Grid: N 95773 36369

This obelisk, commonly known as Conolly's Folly, stands 4km northwest of Castletown House, Celbridge. It was commissioned at a cost of about £500 by Katherine Conolly, the widow of Speaker William Conolly of Castletown House, to provide famine relief after the severe frosts of 1739. Construction workers were paid a halfpenny a day and, in this time of severe famine, the welcome employment was considered a great act of philanthropy. The folly was designed by the architect Richard Castle, who at the time was working for the Earl of Kildare at nearby Carton House. The folly stands 42m high and is composed of a 20m shaft, standing on top of a series of eight arches. The design features a number of stone pineapples, symbols of wealth and hospitality, on the side arches, and carved eagles perching on urns which stand on tall plinths at the side of the obelisk shaft. A narrow staircase runs to a chamber underneath the shaft, where fine views can be had of the distant Dublin Mountains. In the early 1960s, the folly was restored by the Irish Georgian Society with the help of Belfast steeplejacks. Later an early drawing of the folly was adopted as the society's emblem. Under one of the arches can be found the grave of Mariga Guinness, the co-founder of the Irish Georgian Society and first wife of the Honourable Desmond Guinness. The OPW has recently completed further restoration works.

View of folly from west.

Jigginstown House

County Kildare

Map no. 64; GPS: N 53.214026, W 6.683378; Irish Grid: N 88007 18958

In 1636, Thomas Wentworth, Earl of Strafford and Lord Deputy of Ireland, started building Jigginstown House, with the intention of using it as his summer residence. It was also designed to be suitable for Charles I to use as his palace, if he ever visited Ireland. Wentworth, however, would never see the house finished as he was called back to London, accused of high treason, and executed in front of a crowd of 200,000 people on 12 May 1641. Following news of Strafford's execution, Ireland rose in rebellion in October 1641. In 1643, it was at Jigginstown that James Butler, the first Duke of Ormonde, signed the Cessation of Arms with the Catholic Confederates. In his 1820 book *Excursions through Ireland*, Thomas Cromwell credits the construction of the house to a member of the Allen family. It was most likely the architect John Allen, who had come to Ireland from Holland. Tradition relates that the house was built with bricks manufactured in Holland and brought to Dublin by ship. The bricks were then passed hand to hand along an enormous human chain until they reached Jigginstown. The house was vast, measuring about 140m in length, and was one of the first in Ireland to be built of red brick. Little remains above ground; however, the vaulted basements are particularly fine.

Left: View of basement steps.
Below: View of vaulted basement.

Kilteel Castle

County Kildare

Map no. 65; GPS: N 53.232191, W 6.529055; Irish Grid: N 98275 21181

Before his death in 1257, Maurice Fitzgerald, second Baron of Offaly, established a Commandary (or settlement) of the Knights Hospitallers of St John of Jerusalem at Kilteel. In 1335, Robert Clifford was appointed porter to the Commandary. It is recorded that he was supplied with suitable clothing, half a mark annually for shoes, and was given the use of apartments near the castle gate. With the advent of the dissolution of the monasteries, Sir John Rawson, Prior of the Hospital of St John of Jerusalem in Ireland, began to let Hospitaller properties at low rents on long leases. The beneficiaries were often his family members or his political allies. In 1541, he made a grant of the manor of Kilteel to Thomas Alen, brother of the Lord Chancellor, forever, for the rent of £5. By the end of the seventeenth century, the castle had passed to Sir Richard Talbot, Earl of Tyrconnell, who leased it to Daniel Reading. The Earl joined King James's army and died shortly after being defeated in the Battle of the Boyne. His estates were forfeited and in 1703, Kilteel was sold to the Hollow Sword Blade Company, an English company that had diversified from sword manufacturing into land purchase. The castle was later sold to Sir William Fownes. In 1773, it was sold to the Tighe family and in 1838, the Kennedy family. The castle stands a little over 14m high and consists of a five-storey tower, of which the bottom and fourth floors are vaulted, with an attached D-shaped turret containing the spiral staircase and an attached gateway.

View of gateway attached to castle.

Moone High Cross

County Kildare

Map no. 66; GPS: N 52.980173, W 6.825771; Irish Grid: S 78922 92768

Moone High Cross, standing a little over 5m high, is the second tallest high cross in Ireland. The cross was carved in three pieces of granite during the eighth century. The upper part of the cross, and the base were both found buried in the church graveyard in 1835. They were re-erected by the Duke of Leinster in 1850. In 1893, the centre piece of the cross was also discovered, thus allowing the restoration of the complete cross by the Kildare Archaeological Society. As the three stone pieces had been buried for many centuries, they are in a remarkable state of preservation, making the cross amongst the finest in Ireland. The biblical scenes which are represented in the carvings include: The Miracle of Loaves and Fishes and The Flight into Egypt on the north face; The Twelve Apostles and The Crucifixion on the east face; The Temptation of St Anthony and a six-headed beast on the south face; and Daniel in the Lions' Den and the Sacrifice of Isaac on the west face. In 1995, after restoration work at Moone, the cross was cleaned and installed inside the ruined church, along with another highly decorated cross. Roofing panels now provide protection from the elements. The church was built on the site of an ancient monastery, believed to have been founded by St Palladius, who came to Ireland in the year 431. The monastery was later dedicated to St Columcille in the sixth century. The ruined church that stands on the site today was founded by the Fitzgeralds in the thirteenth century and repaired in 1609.

Left: Scene of Daniel in the Lions' Den on west face. **Right:** The Twelve Apostles on east face.

Punchestown Standing Stone

County Kildare

Map no. 67; GPS: N 53.191945, W 6.628017; Irish Grid: N 91752 16571

Punchestown Standing Stone, known locally as the Longstone, stands over 6m high, and is said to be the tallest and most elegant in Ireland. The granite stone tapers finely upwards from its base circumference of about 3m. According to legend the stone was thrown from the Hill of Allen by the great mythical hunter-warrior Fionn MacCumhaill in a test of his strength. Prior to 1934, the stone leant at an angle of about thirty degrees. Legend relates that this slant of the stone was caused by the Viscount Allen's attempt to remove the stone to his mansion house at Punchestown. Apparently he chained up fourteen pairs of oxen to the stone and attempted to drag it from the ground. In 1934, when it was eventually restored to the vertical, an empty Bronze Age stone burial cist was found close to its base.

View of stone face, looking upwards.

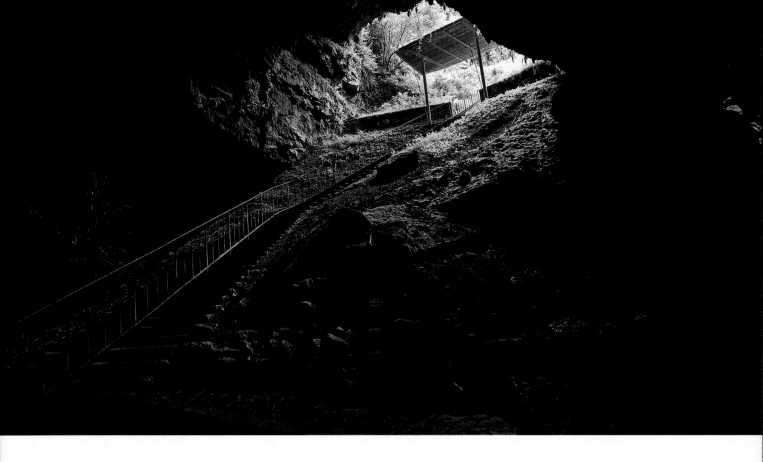

Dunmore Cave

County Kilkenny

Map no. 68; GPS: N 52.734421, W 7.248917; Irish Grid: S 50786 65038

Dunmore is the only cave in Ireland that is in State care. It is formed of limestone laid down over 300 million years ago. The passages of the cave run for about 400m and reach a depth of about 50m. Its entrance, which is 11m wide and 6m high, leads into the Main Chamber and the Fairies' Floor. Legend relates that any object left on the ground here will be cleared away as the fairies use it as their dancefloor and sweep it every night. Other sections of the cave include the Market Cross Chamber, where a huge cross-shaped stalagmite rises to a height of nearly 6m, and the Crystal Hall, where crystal-encrusted stalactites and stalagmites surround a deep, blue pool of water. The earliest reference to the cave is in the Irish Triads where it is listed as one of the three darkest places in Ireland. The most important historical reference is given in the Annals of the Four Masters under the date AD 928, when Vikings are recorded as having massacred 1,000 people who had sought refuge in the cave. Visits by antiquarians in the eighteenth and nineteenth centuries record grim discoveries of vast quantities of human bones, many of which had become encased in calcite over hundreds of years, to form part of the cave structure. Numerous bones were carried off as souvenirs. The cave was designated a National Monument in 1940 and it was later opened to the public. Surveys between 1973 and 1976 removed the bones of nineteen adults and twenty-five children. Radiocarbon dating and analysis of the calcite deposits dated the bones to the period of the Viking attack. A number of Viking coins was also discovered which may have been lost during the gruesome events of the massacre.

Left: View of cave entrance.
Above: View of calcite formations.

Grangefertagh Round Tower
and Church

County Kilkenny

Map no. 69; GPS: N 52.778989, W 7.54529; Irish Grid: S 30734 69830

The first monastic settlement on this site was founded by St Ciarán of Saigir in the sixth century. The Annals of the Four Masters record that it was here, in the year 861, that King Cearbhall of Ossory killed a Viking army and carried away forty of their heads. The Canons Regular of St Augustine later took over the site and founded a priory. Under the dissolution of the monasteries, the monastery was officially suppressed in 1540, when Robert Shortal was prior. The round tower is the only surviving remnant of the early monastery. It has eight floors and stands nearly 33m high. At one time it was the tallest round tower in Ireland but it lost that distinction when its conical cap fell. In 1156, Eochaidh Ua Cuinn, the chief scholar of the monastery, was burnt to death during a raid on the community, when a fire was started at the tower's base. The doorway of the tower retained its original rounded top until the early nineteenth century, when a farmer removed the stonework. He believed the stones to be fireproof, and unsuccessfully installed them as firebricks in his kitchen. A church built next to the tower was

in use until about 1780 and was later converted for use as a handball alley. The better-preserved chapel, to the side of the church, contains the fine Gothic tomb of John Mac Gillapatrick. The tomb was carved about 1540 by Rory O'Tunney and features effigies of Mac Gillapatrick in armour, with his wife by his side. During the nineteenth century, the west doorway and east window of the chapel were removed to Johnstown Church of Ireland, and the baptismal font to Johnstown Catholic Church.

Clockwise from top left: Exterior view of late medieval window; View of tower doorway; View of John Mac Gillapatrick's tomb. (Note architectural patterns on chest sides.); View of tower top (conical top missing).

Jerpoint Abbey

County Kilkenny

Map no. 70; GPS: N 52.511468, W 7.158108; Irish Grid: S 57209 40296

The Cistercian foundation of Jerpoint is among the finest monastic establishments dating from the medieval period in Ireland. Its name is derived from the reference to the abbey in Latin documents as *de Jeriponte*. The exact date of its foundation has been lost to history; however, Donald O Donoghoe, King of Ossory, gave the site to the Cistercians before the Anglo-Norman invasion of 1170 and much of the construction was completed in the latter years of the twelfth century. The oldest parts of the abbey, which may date back as far as 1160, are the transepts and presbytery, though the original east window was replaced in the fourteenth century. The presbytery area contains the tomb of Felix O'Dulany, the first abbot of Jerpoint and Bishop of Ossory, who died in 1202. The nave of the church was divided by a cross-wall, which separated the lay brothers' choir to the west and the monks' choir to the east. In 1228, there were fifty lay brothers and thirty-six monks in residence. The abbey was much improved in the fifteenth century when a crenellated crossing tower and a fine cloister were added. The cloister, which has been much restored, measures about 30m square. Its pillars feature a remarkable number of carvings. At least six knights are depicted in fine armour, as well as courtly damsels and various saints including St Catherine of Alexandria, St Margaret, and St Michael overcoming a dragon. Under the dissolution of the monasteries, Jerpoint Abbey was officially suppressed in March 1540. In 1558, Thomas Butler, the tenth Earl of Ormond, who was also a cousin of Elizabeth I, obtained a grant of the abbey lands, which amounted to nearly 2,000 acres. The abbey was placed into State care in 1880.

Clockwise from above: Carved figure in cloister; View from crossing tower into nave; Felix O'Dulany's tomb in presbytery; View from cloister to crossing tower; View of nave from the cloister.

Killamery High Cross

County Kilkenny

Map no. 71; GPS: N 52.475932, W 7.443838; Irish Grid: S 37841 36154

A monastic settlement was founded at Killamery by St Goban during the seventh century. The first written record is in the Annals of the Four Masters, where the abbot, Domhnall, son of Niall, died in the year 1004. The remains of the monastery, including an ivy-covered arch, were mostly removed in 1815, when the stonework was reused to build the nearby Killamery parish church. A portion of the old chancel wall remained until 1853, when it was demolished and the stones used to build a wall at Killamery police barracks. The parish church survived little more than a century and stands nearby in ruins. The high cross, a ninth-century remnant of the monastery, still stands in its original position. It measures about 3.6m high and 1.2m wide across the arms. The cross and its base are decorated with forty finely carved panels, with subjects ranging from dragons, serpents and other grotesque animals to spirals, marigolds and geometric designs, as well as several scenes. The west face shows a stag-hunting scene, a chariot procession and Adam and Eve after expulsion from Paradise. At the end of the southern arm of the cross is a panel depicting Noah in the Ark and at the northern arm four scenes depicting John the Baptist. The cross has a capstone which was used by locals to treat headaches. An immediate cure was effected by the capstone being temporarily removed from the cross and placed on the patient's head.

View of south face of cross.

Knockroe Passage Tomb

County Kilkenny

Map no. 72; GPS: N 52.431577, W 7.40118; Irish Grid: S 40780 31241

The Knockroe structure comprises a circular cairn, about 20m in diameter, inside which are two separate tombs. The western tomb was entered through a passage from the kerb, while the eastern tomb did not have a passage to the outside. Megalithic art has been recorded on numerous stones in both tombs and also on the kerb which surrounds the cairn. The decoration on the stones is unequalled except, at Knowth (p. 209), Newgrange (p. 210) and Dowth (p. 209) in the Boyne Valley. Excavations carried out in the 1990s revealed that the face of the cairn, especially in the area of the eastern tomb, appeared to have been once decorated with quartz. Another indication that this was a special site is the solar alignment. At nightfall on the winter solstice, the setting sun meets the horizon at a point which aligns directly with the passage of the western tomb. This tomb is divided into three compartments, each separated by a sill stone and floored with a large slab. An artificial platform of boulder clay stretched between the two tombs and at the western tomb's entrance formed a type of forecourt with a façade of sandstone blocks flanking the entrance. Excavation of the forecourt revealed a sizeable fire pit and both the eastern and western tombs contained large amounts of cremated human bone. Other finds included Carrowkeel ware, a mushroom-headed pin, a pendant and a bead.

View of western tomb.
Opposite page: View of megalithic art in eastern tomb.

Knockroe Passage Tomb.

View of entrance to keep: stonework
possibly inserted from elsewhere in the
eighteenth century. (Note: the carving
on left and right of arch-head stones is
subtly different, perhaps indicating they
were originally from different doors.)

Dunamase Castle

County Laois

Map no. 73; GPS: N 53.031613, W 7.209435; Irish Grid: S 53089 98140

The Rock of Dunamase is over 44m high and dominates the surrounding plain, making it an ideal natural defensive position. The first structure on the site was an early Christian fort, from which the site derives its name *Dún Masc* or 'the fort of Masc'. The castle was later built in stages, and comprises a keep, an inner ward, middle ward and outer ward, with an outer bailey further to the southeast. Access to the outer bailey is through a barbican gatehouse and to the middle ward by a gate-tower. The castle's founder is not recorded but is likely to be Strongbow, William Marshal, or Meiler FitzHenry. FitzHenry probably built the keep and inner ward in the 1180s and was in possession of the castle until his defeat in 1208, after which William Marshal took control. Marshal then added the middle and outer wards, and numerous loops for shooting arrows. The castle passed to Marshal's youngest daughter Eva, and then to Eva's eldest daughter Maud, who married Roger Mortimer, Baron Wigmore. Their grandson, also called Roger, was appointed Lord Lieutenant of Ireland in 1316. He took Queen Isabella, wife of Edward II, as his mistress and in 1330 was condemned for high treason, and then hanged, drawn and quartered. His estates were forfeited to the Crown and the castle was abandoned around this time. Three hundred years later, Cromwell's troops made sure the castle could never be reused, by blowing up its walls with gunpowder. In 1795, Sir John Parnell started to convert the keep for use as a banqueting hall, but he died in 1801, leaving the project unfinished.

Killeshin Church

County Laois

Map no. 74; GPS: N 52.84748, W 7.001424; Irish Grid: S 67329 77823

A monastic settlement was founded here by St Comghan towards the end of the fifth century. Other saints connected with the location are St Aedhan who died in 843 and St Diarmaid who was the abbot in 874. The settlement was raided in 1041, at which time an oratory was destroyed. The monastery was then burnt in 1077. The church, which survives today in ruins, was built in two stages. The west walls, including the Romanesque doorway and adjoining parts of the side walls, were built in the twelfth century and the east end in the fifteenth century. The Romanesque doorway has four orders and is amongst the finest in Ireland. It stands over 5m high, with the opening about 2m high and 1m wide. It is built of three different types of stone: a fine-grained brown sandstone, a coarse yellow granite and light-coloured granite. At some point, the doorway was rebuilt and the stones forming the pilasters and arch no longer sit in their original positions. The doorway is decorated with foliage designs and animals including a stag, representing Christ, a manticore (with the head of a man, body of a lion and tail of a scorpion) representing death, and a griffin, thought to represent the devil carrying off the souls of sinners. A 32m-high round tower once stood to the northwest of the church. This was demolished on 8 March 1703, under the instruction of the local landowner, who feared that it might fall on his cattle.

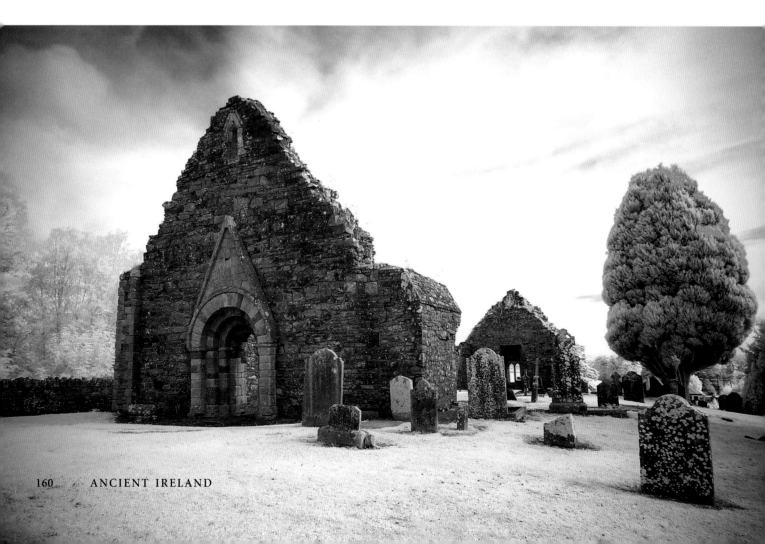

Clockwise from top left:
External view of fifteenth-century
east window; Detail of carving on
outer order of Romanesque doorway;
External view of window in north wall;
View of church interior looking west.

Timahoe Round Tower

County Laois

Map no. 75; GPS: N 52.960447, W 7.203856; Irish Grid: S 53551 90224

The first monastic settlement was founded here in the seventh century by St Mochua, a hermit who was assisted in his vigils by his three pets: a cockerel, a mouse and a fly. The cockerel would wake him if he dozed off, whilst the mouse would nibble at his ear, not letting him sleep more than three hours during the night. The fly would walk along each line of his Psalms, pausing if the saint became tired, so he could continue again reading from the same word. The settlement was raided and the oratory burnt in 919 and again in 1142. The round tower is the only surviving remnant of this early monastery. It stands nearly 30m tall and has walls nearly 2m thick. It has six storeys, with four large windows facing the cardinal points at the top. The Romanesque doorway is by far the most elaborate of any round tower in Ireland. It comprises two doorways, one behind the other, and has four steps which lead into the second storey of the tower. Its pilasters are decorated with human heads whose flowing hair is formed into varying patterns. A second doorway was later inserted at ground level, but after the tower started to

lean to the northwest, with its top moving more than half a metre, this was quickly filled in. The ruined building next to the tower began as a fifteenth-century church. After the dissolution of the monasteries, the monastery lands were granted to Sir Thomas Loftus and later Richard Cosby, whose son had married Loftus's daughter. A member of this family rebuilt the church, fortifying it to become a castle, in which Loftus died in 1635. It appears that friars remained at Timahoe until they were killed by Cromwell's soldiers in 1650.

Clockwise from top left: View of decorated, church, stonework, now concealed in the castle wall; View of tower doorway; Remains of the church, later converted to a castle; View of round tower from east.

Corracloona Court Tomb

County Leitrim

Map no. 76; GPS: N 54.334343, W 8.004055; Irish Grid: G 99785 42845

This court tomb is unique in Ireland, being the only example of a tomb with a porthole or kennel-hole entrance. Whether this entrance was deliberately carved or if it resulted from a natural break in the stone remains unclear. The tomb was excavated in July 1953 and was found to be badly disturbed and in a very ruinous condition. Local tradition related that it was once covered by a cairn which rose to a height of 4m, but at the time of the excavation most of the cairn had disappeared, seemingly a result of the site being used as a stone quarry when the nearby road was constructed during the years of the Great Famine. The excavation revealed a single, centrally placed chamber 3.5m long and 2.5m wide, with a V-shaped forecourt. The cairn reached a height of about 1.5m and was surrounded by a kerb. Finds included pottery sherds and a number of flints. Local tradition calls the tomb both 'Prince Connell's Grave' and 'Grave of the Great Gallagher'. Apparently it was named after a 'Donegal marauder who received due justice at the hands of the good people of Leitrim'.

Top: View of site from northeast. **Below:** View through porthole entrance to tomb interior.

Creevelea Friary

County Leitrim

Map no. 77; GPS: N 54.231161, W 8.309634; Irish Grid: G 79856 31403

Creevelea Friary was founded for the Franciscans in 1508 by Owen O'Rourke and his wife, Margaret O'Brien. It was the last Franciscan friary to be founded in Ireland before the dissolution of the monasteries. The cloister and domestic buildings are to the north of the church instead of the usual south, perhaps to take advantage of the fine view over the River Bonet. In the cloister, there are three interesting carvings on one of the cloister bays near the middle of the north side. One shows St Francis marked with the stigmata, the second a foliage pattern, and the third St Francis standing in a pulpit with birds perched on a nearby tree, referring to the legend that he could speak the language of birds. Another curious feature in the cloister is the many single carved letters. Unfortunately the meaning of the letters has been lost as many of the pillars fell and were not re-erected in their original positions. In 1536, the friary was partly destroyed by an accidental fire. One of the friars, Heremon O'Donnell, perished in the flames whilst trying to save some sacred vessels. Bryan O'Rourke began the work of restoration but this was never completed and the friary was suppressed in 1539. About 1590, Sir Richard Bingham converted the church into a stable for his soldiers' horses. In 1617, Captain Walter Harrison was granted the friary lands. He erected a gate at the entrance to the friary cemetery and charged locals large sums of money for burials within its hallowed grounds. Five friars were allowed to cover part of the church with a thatched roof and the community remained there in fairly miserable conditions until the end of the seventeenth century.

Above: View of chancel to east window. **Top right:** View of cloister. **Bottom right:** Carving of St Francis in a pulpit with birds perched on a nearby tree.

Fenagh Churches

County Leitrim

Map no. 78; GPS: N 54.01894, W 7.835612; Irish Grid: H 10824 07749

St Caillin founded a monastic settlement at Fenagh during the sixth century. Legend relates that he was subsequently visited by St Patrick, and presented with the *Clog-na-Righ* or Bell of Kings, which had many mystical powers. Unfortunately the bell and also the priceless St Caillin's book shrine were destroyed in 2009 when the museum that housed them burnt down. The Book of Fenagh, which contains verse and prose about the life of St Caillin and was published in the nineteenth century, thankfully endures. What survives on this monastic site today are the remains of two roofless churches, surrounded by a number of earthworks. The church at the south, which adjoins a modern graveyard, measures about 26m long by 7m wide. The west end of the church has a barrel vault above which was space that may have been used for accommodation. The vaulted area later became the burial place for the Lawder family. At the east end of the church, the hood moulding of the fine fourteenth- or fifteenth-century window is decorated with human heads at both ends and the apex. Just below the window, an unusual string coursing is terminated with animal figures. The church further to the north measures about 19m long by 6m wide. It was probably built in the fifteenth century, partly reusing stone from an earlier church. The monastery was suppressed in 1541 and in 1585, the lands were transferred to the Protestant Bishop of Ardagh. The larger church continued to be used for worship until the nearby Church of Ireland was built around 1800.

Clockwise from top:
Interior view of the north church looking west; Head carved on kneeler of east gable; View through barrel vault of the south church towards east window.

Parke's Castle

County Leitrim

Map no. 79; GPS: N 54.264698, W 8.334332; Irish Grid: G 78263 35144

An earlier castle on the site was a stronghold of the O'Rourke family from the twelfth century. In 1591, Sir Brian O'Rourke, was captured by the English and taken to London to be hanged for his support of the Spanish Armada. At this time the castle comprised a fifteenth-century tower house surrounded by a bawn. After his death, O'Rourke's lands were granted to Captain Robert Parke. Parke demolished the tower house, using the stone to build a three-storey, semi-fortified manor house, which was built into the eastern side of the bawn. The north side of the bawn featured a round flanking tower at either end, one of which was incorporated into the house. A turret on the southern corner looks out over Lough Gill. During the seventeenth century, the water level is thought to have been about 3m higher than the current level, so water lapped up against the bawn walls. A sally port (a fortified water gateway) provided access from the bawn to the lough. Robert Parke died in 1671, leaving the castle to his daughter, Anne, who married Sir Francis Gore. The family abandoned the castle early in the eighteenth century and by the start of the nineteenth century it was already in ruins. Francis and Anne's great grandson later build Lissadell House in County Sligo, home of revolutionary Constance Gore-Booth (Countess Markievicz). Parke's Castle was vested into State care and carefully restored by the OPW during the 1990s. Window glazing was replaced and the timber stairs, floors and roof beams were rebuilt using traditional techniques and craftsmanship of the seventeenth century. A well-preserved sweat house located just west of the castle makes an interesting detour.

Top: View of castle from east.
Left: Interior view of castle gallery.

Duntryleague Passage Tomb

County Limerick

Map no. 80; GPS: N 52.405796, W 8.321543; Irish Grid: R 78166 28252

Located near the top of Duntryleague Hill, this is one of the few Neolithic passage tombs in the south of Ireland, and the only one in County Limerick. Duntryleague derives its name from the Irish *Dún Trí Liag*, or Fort of Three Pillar Stones. On the first edition Ordinance Survey map, the tomb is marked as 'Dermot & Grania's Bed', recording the site as a rest place of the legendary couple, during their flight from the angry Fionn MacCumhaill. The High King Cormac mac Airt had promised his daughter, Grania/Gráinne, as a bride for Fionn, but instead she ran away with Dermot/Diarmuid. Fionn later exacted his revenge by failing to heal Diarmuid when he was gored by a wild boar. Folklore also identifies the tomb as the grave of Olioll Olum, a King of Munster who died in 234. Remains of the cairn are not evident but the passage and chamber survive reasonably intact. The tomb is orientated north to south, with the entrance at the north, suggesting no particular solar or lunar alignment. The 6m-long passage leads to a chamber at the southern end, measuring about 3m by 1.5m, which is still covered by capstones. The remains of two further chambers can be seen, one on either side of the passage, about halfway along its length.

View from tomb chamber.

Grange Stone Circle

Grange Stone Circle

County Limerick

Map no. 81; GPS: N 52.514288, W 8.541774; Irish Grid: R 63268 40414

The impressive stone circle at Grange is located south of Lough Gur and is one of a large group of prehistoric monuments. It consists of a ring of 113 stones enclosing a level surface approximately 46m in diameter which is higher than the surrounding ground level. Unusually, the stones are set against a broad flat-topped bank roughly the same height as the stones. A narrow stone-lined entrance cuts through this bank on the northeast side and large portal stones are found on either side of the interior of the entrance. Work was carried out on the monument at various times in the nineteenth century by the landlord Count de Salis and his tenants John and Edward Fitzgerald. Evidence from an excavation carried out in 1939 and the testimony of John O'Donovan, one of the workmen employed on the excavation, who had also worked on the circle for Mr Fitzgerald, revealed that the bank had been repaired in places and smaller stones inserted as packing between the larger orthostats. The site had a ritual function and it has been suggested that the bank could have been used for spectators to view proceedings in the interior. The excavation revealed a post-hole in the very centre of the circle, two hearths on the old ground level and another hearth under the bank. Finds included flint and chert implements, stone axes, three bronze objects, some human and animal bone and thousands of pieces of Late Neolithic/Early Bronze Age pottery. The site is usually dated to this period but a re-evaluation of the pottery in 2004 has suggested it may be a Late Bronze Age monument built on a site of prolonged use.

Kilmallock Abbey

County Limerick

Map no. 82; GPS: N 52.402537, W 8.574829; Irish Grid: R 60925 27996

The Dominican priory at Kilmallock was founded by Gilbert, son of Lord Offaly, in 1291, whose family, a branch of the Fitzgeralds, were to become the FitzGibbons (the White Knights). The grave slab of Edmund, the last White Knight, who died in 1608, lies in the chancel. The buildings are in good condition with some fine examples of decorative carving and evidence of several building phases. The church, with the claustral buildings to the north, was originally a simple nave-and-chancel church but a south transept and nave aisle were added in the early fourteenth century. In the fifteenth century a tower was added, and alterations were carried out to the cloister arcade and north range. The beautiful early Gothic east chancel window has five graded lights, divided by slender mullions. Early-fourteenth-century sculptural motifs, such as ball-flower decoration, used in the south transept are examples of the Late Decorated style and suggest that the mason had recently worked in the English West Country. Unusual 'Atlas' figures, with arms held aloft, protrude from the transept walls, to support the double

transept arcade. Several other well-carved human heads can be seen on window arches and tomb niches. The well-preserved five-light reticulated window in the southern wall of the transept was restored in the late nineteenth century by the Royal Society of Antiquaries of Ireland. The abbey and its lands were leased in the sixteenth century but the friars had returned by 1639, when a silver chalice was given to the priory by Callaghan O'Callaghan and his wife. One of four inscriptions asks for a prayer for Maurice Gibbon, presumably the son of the last White Knight, who died the day before his father. The abbey was fully abandoned about 1790.

Clockwise from top left: View from chancel to west door; View of Atlas figure protruding from transept wall; View of fine tomb in chancel; View of cloister.

King John's Castle

County Limerick

Map no. 83; GPS: N 52.669811, W 8.625576; Irish Grid: R 57729 57767

This imposing castle, known as King John's, lies on the western side of King's Island. It was built in the early thirteenth century by the Anglo-Normans to protect the crossing point to Thomond. Partly built on an earlier twelfth-century ringwork, the castle lay to the north of the original Viking settlement known as Ostman and was incorporated into Limerick's growing city walls. The castle was a royal castle in the care of the king's representative and, like Dublin Castle, does not have a keep but consists of a curtain wall enclosing a courtyard with large circular towers at three corners and a large angular bastion at the southeastern corner, which replaced a small tower about 1611. The entrance on the northern side is flanked by two D-shaped towers. Over the centuries the castle has been neglected, repaired, put under siege, taken and retaken several times. In 1787, a barracks was built in the courtyard so continuing its military function, until corporation houses were constructed in the 1930s. The latest addition to the structure was the interpretative centre which allows the visitor to view the underground area excavated in the 1990s. These excavations uncovered evidence of the 1642 siege of the castle by the Confederates and reveals a tale

of high drama, secrecy, death and eventual victory for the besiegers. The tunnels used to undermine the walls of the castle were found with well-preserved wooden props and side-wall lining planks still in place. The inside story was recorded in a diary written almost certainly by the cleric Ambrose Jones. The following extract records the moment the bastion was breached on 17 June: 'This morning was perceived a great cracke in the bulwarke of our castle from the top to ye bottome which before we doubted to be undermined …'.

Clockwise from top: Interior view of castle entrance; King John – deep in thought?; View along curtain walls to entrance tower.

Granard Motte

County Longford

Map no. 84; GPS: N 53.77545, W 7.500701; Irish Grid: N 32968 80751

Granard Motte was constructed in 1199 by Sir Richard de Tuite, an Anglo-Norman knight who was invited into Longford by the Lords of Cairbre to provide military assistance. The motte is thought to be the tallest in Ireland. It was formed by digging a circular fosse into a natural hillock, with the excavated rock and soil being deposited on the top, forming a steep 10m-high mound. A castle, constructed of timber, would have been built on the mound's flat top. On the south side there are the remains of a large D-shaped bailey, surrounded by a second fosse and massive earth banks. In 1211, Sir Richard de Tuite was accidently killed at Athlone by a falling tower. His remains lie a few miles away in the Cistercian abbey at Abbeylara. It is thought that a few years later, King John stayed here during his campaign to suppress Hugh de Lacy. The motte subsequently became the inauguration place of the Ó Fearghail clan. In 1475, Seán Ó Fearghail died on the motte immediately after his inauguration feast. He was also buried at Abbeylara. Today the summit of the motte is occupied by an OS trigonometrical station and a statue of St Patrick, which was erected in 1932. There are many legends concerning the motte. One tells of headless horsemen guarding the way to concealed treasures. Apparently, around 1787, a hole was dug into its side, revealing the well-built arched vaults of a castle. Whether or not there are any internal secrets remains a mystery, as the motte has never been excavated. Fine panoramic views, which stretch across County Longford and into counties Westmeath and Cavan, can be seen from its peak.

View of motte from southwest.

Inchcleraun Island Monastic Site

County Longford

Map no. 85; GPS: N 53.58229, W 8.006265; Irish Grid: M 99634 59135

Inchcleraun Island, or in Irish, *Inis Cloithrin*, according to legend derives its name from its first inhabitant, Cloithrin, sister of Queen Maeve. The story relates that the queen was killed on the island by a stone fired from a catapult on the shoreline 2km away. The assassin, Forbuidhe, seemingly practised the shot for a year and a day. A monastic settlement was later founded on the island by St Diarmuid in the sixth century. The Annals of the Four Masters record the settlement being plundered by 'the men of Munster' several times during the eleventh century. During the twelfth century, the island's inhabitants adopted the rule of St Augustine and a priory church dedicated to St Mary was built. This is probably Templemore, one of a group of six churches located on the island, which include the Church of the Dead, Templedermot, Templemurry and the Women's Church. A curious local superstition relates that any woman who enters Templemurry will meet her death twelve months later. *Clogás an Oileáin,* or the bell-tower church of the island, dates from the early thirteenth century. It stands alone, crowning the island's highest point. The unusual square tower at its west end is unique in Ireland for a church of this period; however, there are similar Anglo-Saxon examples in England. The Augustinian priory was suppressed in 1541 after the dissolution of the monasteries. During the nineteenth century the island became known as Quaker's Island, after the Fairbrother family who took up residence. Inchcleraun received some international press attention in the 1990s when ancient gravestones stolen from the island were offered for sale to a Boston College for $435,000. Following an investigation by the National Museum of Ireland and the Federal Bureau of Investigation the perpetrator was apprehended and the artefacts returned to Ireland.

Left: Interior view of *Clogás an Oileáin* square tower.
Right: Interior view of Templemore looking towards west window.
Below: Interior view of Templemurry looking towards east window.

Castleroche Castle

County Louth

Map no. 86; GPS: N 54.046477, W 6.488693; Irish Grid: H 99043 11860

Castleroche sits spectacularly on top of a large, precipitous outcrop of natural rock, which protects it on all sides, except on the east where there is a rock-cut fosse. It is thought that the castle was built by Rohesia de Verdon, in 1236, a few years after the death of her first husband, Theobald le Botiller (Butler). Legend has it that Rohesia had such a bad temper that architects were not willing to work for her and she resorted to offering her hand in marriage to the man who would build her castle. When complete, the architect was asked to survey his fine work from an upstairs window, and then promptly pushed out to his death on the rocks below. Rohesia died in 1245 and it is thought work on the castle was continued by her son, John. The castle was approached over a drawbridge across the fosse on the eastern side. The gatehouse comprises two towers, rounded at the front, but squared off at the rear. The towers provided considerable living space on two floors above the entranceway. To the southwest of the gatehouse there was a large hall, with the first-floor level lit by three large windows in the outer wall. The projecting tower at the northern corner of the castle is now very ruinous, but once also provided considerable living space over four storeys. There was no keep inside the castle, so its strength lay totally in the surrounding curtain walls and gatehouse. In 1366, John Bellew bought out the de Verdon interests in County Louth and in 1464, his grandson Richard obtained state grants for the repair of the castle. In 1561, all English forces in Ireland gathered at Castleroche, prior to marching into Ulster in the pursuit of Shane O'Neill.

Top: View of remains of gatehouse from castle interior.
Left: External view of gatehouse.
Right: View of castle interior.

COUNTY LOUTH: CASTLEROCHE CASTLE   185

Clochafarmore Standing Stone

County Louth

Map no. 87; GPS: N 53.974919, W 6.466999; Irish Grid: J 00637 03926

This standing stone is located in a lonely field in the townland of Rathiddy, about 1km from the village of Knockbridge. The stone measures over 3m high and more than 1m wide. Its name, Clochafarmore, is derived from the Irish *Cloch an Fhir Mhóir* which translates as 'The Great Man's Stone'. Tradition relates that this is where the legendary warrior hero Cúchulainn met his death. One account goes that Cúchulainn had been mortally wounded by a spear thrown by his enemy Lugaid. Wanting to face his enemies and his death standing up, Cúchulainn tied himself to the Clochafarmore Standing Stone. As he took his final breaths, his horse, the Grey of Macha, trying to protect his master, made three attacks on Lugaid's army, killing fifty men with its teeth, and thirty with each of its hooves. Finally a raven came and settled on Cúchulainn's shoulders and Lugaid knew he was dead. He lifted up Cúchulainn's hair from his shoulders, and struck off his head. Cúchulainn's sword fell from his arm, severing Lugaid's hand. In the 1920s a bronze spearhead was found close to the standing stone. It was given to the parish priest for safekeeping but today its whereabouts is unknown. In 1935, a statue, 'The Death of Cúchulainn', was unveiled in the General Post Office in Dublin, as a memorial to the participants of the 1916 Easter Rising.

View of stone face, looking upwards.

Mellifont Abbey

County Louth

Map no. 88; GPS: N 53.74229, W 6.466248; Irish Grid: O 01246 78037

The architecturally influential monastery of Mellifont, the first Cistercian abbey in Ireland, was founded by St Malachy, Archbishop of Armagh, in 1142, on lands granted by Donough O'Carroll, Prince of Louth. The mother house was Clairvaux Abbey in northeast France. Some Irishmen were trained at Clairvaux, before returning with French monks and a skilled architect, named Robert, to form the new Cistercian community in Ireland. The abbey church was consecrated in a grand ceremony in 1157. Attendees included 18 bishops; Murtough MacLoughlainn, the most powerful king in Ireland, who gave 140 cows and 60 ounces of gold; O'Carroll, Prince of Louth who also gave 60 ounces of gold; and Tiernan O'Rourke, King of Breifne, and his wife Dervorgilla, who gave another 60 ounces of gold together with a chalice for the altar. By 1170, the abbey contained more than 100 monks and 300 lay brothers. When it was dissolved in 1539, the community comprised just 21 monks. Mellifont was granted to Sir Edward Moore, who transformed the abbey into a fine fortified mansion, where his descendants resided until 1727. The Moores became Earls and then Marquesses of Drogheda and moved to another former Cistercian monastery

at Monasterevin, County Kildare, which was renamed Moore Abbey. Mellifont appears to have then become used as a quarry, with much sold off and removed. Statues of the twelve apostles found a new home at Moore Abbey and a large mill built nearby in the late eighteenth century reused much of the abbey stonework. The surviving remains are rather meagre, but include the early-thirteenth-century octagonal lavabo and chapterhouse, the late medieval gatehouse and a section of the Romanesque cloister arcade, which was re-erected in 1955. Excavations have revealed the church, which was remodelled on several occasions, and several other buildings, but they survive only as pillar bases and wall foundations.

Left: View through lavabo to abbey remains. **Top:** View of medieval gatehouse. **Above:** View towards the lavabo from the west end of the church. Walls in foreground are part of a crypt.

Monasterboice

County Louth

Map no. 89; GPS: N 53.777656, W 6.417282; Irish Grid: O 04389 82044

A monastic settlement was founded here by St Buithe or Boecius at the start of the sixth century. It derives its name from the Latin *Monasterium Boecii* or 'the monastery of Boecius'. The saint subsequently travelled to Italy and then to Scotland, where it is said that he raised the son of King Nectan back from the dead. Little is known about the history of Monasterboice, except a long list of its abbots and some records of its famous monk, Flann Mainistrech, to whom seven poems are attributed in the Book of Leinster. The monastery remained in existence until at least 1122, after which its importance dwindled, probably due to the rise of the nearby Mellifont Abbey. The importance of the site lies mainly in two of the finest high crosses to be found in Ireland. The Cross of Muiredach, located near the site entrance, stands about 5.5m high. Its name comes from an inscription on its base *OR DO MUIREDACH LASNDERNAD IN CHROS* or 'A prayer for Muiredach by whom the cross was made'. This is possibly Muiredach MacDomnaill, who was abbot in the year 890 and died in 923. In 1898, a moulding of the cross was made and

castings then created were sent to the Victoria and Albert Museum in London, The Metropolitan Museum of Art in New York and to Cardinal Moran in Sydney, Australia, among others. The West Cross, standing near the round tower, is 6.5m high, making it the tallest high cross in Ireland. The round tower, which reaches a height of over 30m, was burned in 1097. Many precious manuscripts and other treasures were destroyed in the blaze. Amongst the other remains at the site are two small medieval churches and two early grave slabs.

Top: Crucifixion scene on west face of Cross of Muiredach. **Left:** View of 'Christ Mocked by the Soldiers' and inscription on Cross of Muiredach base.
Right: View of round tower.

Proleek Tombs

County Louth

Map no. 90; GPS: N 54.03719, W 6.348939; Irish Grid: J 08221 11031

Located beside a golf course at the Ballymascanlan Hotel, within about 80m of each other, are two tombs. A path to them leads from the hotel car park across the golf course. To the east is a wedge tomb, comprising a gallery about 6m long, 1.5m wide at the west and narrowing to 1.1m wide at the east. A large septal stone closes the gallery on the west end, each side of the gallery is formed with eight stones, and the backstone is covered by a single remaining roofstone. To the west is a fine portal tomb, comprising two portal stones, a backstone that is buttressed by a modern stone-and-concrete support, and a massive capstone. The portal stones stand over 2m high with the chamber facing northwest. The enormous capstone measures about 3m wide by 4m long and has been estimated to weigh about forty tons. There are always many stones on top of the capstone as folklore relates that a wish will be granted to anybody who throws a stone on top of the capstone that does not roll off. Early maps show the wedge tomb as 'Giant's Grave' and the portal tomb is known locally as the Giant's Load. Legend tells that the portal tomb was brought from neighbouring mountains and laid in position by the Scottish giant, Para buidhe mór Mhac Seoidin, who came to challenge Fionn MacCumhaill. It is said that the Scottish giant was poisoned by MacCumhaill and lies buried in a grave under the wedge tomb. Folklore relates that several bones of monstrous size were at one time removed from the tomb.

Above: View of wedge tomb from south.
Left: Proleek Portal Tomb.
Opposite page: View of rocks on top of the capstone; perhaps many wishes granted.

COUNTY LOUTH: PROLEEK TOMBS 193

Proleek wedge tomb.

Carrowcrom Tomb

County Mayo

Map no. 91; GPS: N 54.088597, W 9.048271; Irish Grid: G 31452 15998

The well-preserved Carrowcrom Tomb is located in pastureland, southwest of the village of Bunnyconnellan. It retains its single, 2m-long capstone and most of its cairn. The gallery entrance is about 1.5m wide and is flanked on each side by a short façade. The length of the gallery is about 3.5m. Four orthostats at each side of the gallery are visible from the entrance. They start at a height of about 1m and become shorter towards the rear of the gallery. Early maps show the tomb marked as 'Dermot & Grania's Bed'. According to legend, Dermot and Grania (or Diarmuid and Gráinne) were two illicit lovers who eloped and travelled through Ireland for sixteen years, sleeping in a different place every night – hence the large number of Dermot and Grania's Beds throughout the country!

Moyne Friary

County Mayo

Map no. 92; GPS: N 54.202341, W 9.17706; Irish Grid: G 23236 28791

Moyne Friary derives its name from its position at the mouth of the River Moy, overlooking Bartra Island. Permission was given for its construction by Pope Nicholas about 1460. It was founded by MacWilliam Burke, for the Observantine Franciscans, a particularly disciplined branch of the Franciscan order. The church was consecrated in 1462 with building work continuing for many more years. The well-preserved cloister, which is amongst the finest in Ireland, was added at the end of the fifteenth century. The buildings surrounding the cloister include a sacristy and a chapter house next to the church, and on the side opposite of the church, a kitchen and refectory, under which a stream flows facilitating the *necessarium* (toilets). The friars remained at Moyne long after the dissolution of the monasteries. In May 1582, the elderly friar, Felim O'Hara, would not reveal the hiding place for some sacred vessels and was consequently murdered in front of the altar by marauding English soldiers. He was acknowledged as a martyr, and was venerated and beatified by Pope John Paul II in the 1990s. Moyne

Friary was raided in 1578, but remained intact until 1590, when it was set on fire by Sir Richard Bingham, Governor of Connacht. With the community of friars then dispersed, it was leased to Edmund Barrett in 1595, for the annual rent of five shillings. By 1606, it was in the hands of an English widow who let the church and a few rooms, which were all still standing in good order, to six friars. About 1750, the friary was dismantled by the Lindsay family who, it is said, blew up the roof with gunpowder and sold the church bell, which had been a gift to the friars from the Queen of Spain, for the hefty sum of £700.

Clockwise from top left: View from crossing tower to west door; View from south transept to chapel on left with nave in background; View of cloister; View of cloister from first floor.

Rosserk Friary

County Mayo

Map no. 93; GPS: N 54.171466, W 9.143372; Irish Grid: G 25379 25318

Rosserk Friary was founded by the Joyce family around 1440 for a community of Third Order Regular Franciscans. The friary was built on the site of a much earlier church, which had been dedicated to the holy woman Searka, and derives its name from the wooded promontory, or in Irish, *Ros*, on which it stood (hence *Ros Searka*, which later became Rosserk). The friary, built in a bluish-grey stone, is one of the finest and best preserved of the Franciscan friaries in Ireland. The fine Gothic doorway at the western side, facing inland, leads into the wide nave. A tall bell tower divides the nave from the chancel and the eastern window of the chancel features fine, elaborate tracery. On the south wall of the chancel is an unusual double piscina, with a round tower carved on one of its pillars. The rectangular south transept features another fine tracery window and houses an unusual stone confession box, in which two priests could sit, with a hole on each side, through which penitents whispered their sorrows. A very similar stone confession box can also be found at the nearby Moyne Friary. The domestic parts of the friary are joined to the church's north wall. The barrel-vaulted rooms each side of the fine cloister probably served as classrooms or workshops for the friars and the rooms on the upper level were used for sleeping, cooking and eating. Rosserk was attacked and burnt by Sir Richard Bingham, Governor of Connacht, in 1590, the same year in which he also attacked Moyne Friary. By 1603 the roof of the church had fallen in and the friary was in total dereliction.

Top: View of angel carvings on double piscina.
Left: View of Gothic west door.
Right: Stone confession box in south transept.

Strade Abbey

County Mayo

Map no. 94; GPS: N 53.921388, W 9.129059; Irish Grid: M 25869 97469

Strade Abbey, originally known as the Abbey of Athletan, was founded for the Franciscans early in the thirteenth century. It was transferred by Jordan de Exeter in 1252 to the Dominicans when Basilia, wife of Jordan's son, Stephen de Exeter, insisted on replacing the Franciscans with a Dominican order. She apparently organised a great banquet, invited her father, and then refused to eat or drink until her demands for the abbey were agreed to. A messenger was promptly sent to the Pope with a large sum of money and the transfer of the abbey to the Dominicans was soon confirmed. The chancel of the church dates from the thirteenth century; however, work carried out under Pope Eugene IV in 1434 saw much of the building restored and repaired. A sculptured tomb with a Gothic tracery canopy, in the north wall of the chancel, is amongst the finest in Ireland. The tomb front is divided into two sections by a pilaster. On the left three kings, who are probably the magi from the East carrying their gifts of gold, frankincense and myrrh, can be seen standing to the left of Jesus. On the right, two of the figures represent Saints Peter and Paul. The third figure, a bishop, holds a cross in his left hand, and is seen blessing a kneeling figure, who is holding his hood back as a sign of respect. In 1786, the antiquarian Mervyn Archdall

recorded in his *Monasticon Hibernicum* that there was a high altar next to this tomb; this is, however, no longer present. Following the dissolution of the monasteries, Strade was leased to James Garvey in 1578 and Patrick Barnewall in 1588. In 1756 there were seven priests living in a house they had built next to the abbey. Fr Patrick D. Kelly, the last of the friars of Strade died about 1856.

Left: Exterior view of transept window. **Top:** View of very fine sculptured tomb in chancel. **Above:** Internal view to remains of east window.

The Gods of the Neale

County Mayo

Map no. 95; GPS: N 53.573951, W 9.224514; Irish Grid: M 18932 58904

Just east of the village of The Neale, close to the ruins of Lord Kilmaine's house, lies an intriguing stone monument. It is known as 'The Gods of the Neale' and consists of a monument, erected by Kilmaine, which enshrines an ancient stone slab that had been discovered in a nearby cave in 1739. The slab bears carvings of three figures: a dragon, a cow or horse and an angel holding a shield. A plinth carries a much weathered inscription, possibly: '*ORATE PRO AIA MOAINCUS QUI INIUR*' of which a translation has been suggested as 'Pray for the Soul of Moaincus who made me'. Kilmaine inserted a much larger stone slab below the carved figures with the following inscription:

The Irish characters on the above stone import that in this cave we have by us the Gods of Cons:-
Lett us follow their stepps sick of love with full confidencin Loo Lave Adda vackene the shepherd of Ireland of his errand. These images were found in a cave behind the place they now stand and were the

ancient Gods of the Neale which took its name from them they were called Diane FFeale or the gods of Felicity from which the place in Irish was called Ne Heale in English the Neale LL reignd AM 2577 PD 927 Ahte C 1496 and was then: 60 : CEDNA Reignd AM 2994 & 64 of Edna was we; 50 Con Mol was ye son of Heber who divided this kingdom with his brother and had the western parts of this island for his lott all which was originally called from Con Conovent or cons portion and his son Loo Laveadda who found the druids was thought to have drawn all his knowledge from the SVN thus the Irish History. NB the smaller letters on the upper part of the great plinth import that it was erected by Edna Loos Gods were adopted by Con and Edna of the line of Heber established their worship here 1753

It has never been discovered whether the monument contains some mystical wisdom or whether it was in fact a hoax by Lord Kilmaine.

View of slab carvings.

Bective Abbey

County Meath

Map no. 96; GPS: N 53.582595, W 6.702583; Irish Grid: N 85978 59953

Bective Abbey was founded for the Cistercians by Murchad O'Maeil-Sheachlainn, King of Meath, in 1147. It was colonised by monks from Mellifont, County Louth, becoming their first daughter house, and the second Cistercian abbey in Ireland. Bective was never a wealthy house and little of its history is known. The body of Hugh de Lacy, Lord of Meath, killed in 1186 (it is said by one blow of an axe which decapitated him), was buried at Bective, whilst his head was placed in the Abbey of St Thomas in Dublin. A long dispute followed between the two abbeys until, in 1205, his body was removed from Bective and reunited with its head in Dublin. Following the dissolution of the monasteries, the abbey was suppressed in 1536. The last abbot, John Englishe, presided over a church, hall, cloister and other buildings, over 245 acres of land, a water mill and fishing weir. The abbey passed through a number of owners, and was remodelled as a mansion house, with the addition of fireplaces, large mullioned windows and chimneys. It was bought by Sir Richard Bolton, Lord Chancellor of Ireland, in 1639. In the early nineteenth century, the Bolton family built a modern mansion house north of the abbey. The abbey remained in their hands until a relative, Rev. George Martin, placed it into State care in 1894. Nothing remains of the original twelfth-century monastery. The south arcade of the church, now blocked in, was built *c.* 1274 and is the earliest surviving part of the structure. The cloister, which was used by a film crew for a scene in the film *Braveheart*, and other domestic buildings were totally rebuilt in the Late Middle Ages, with the tower being also added at this time.

Above: View of cloister.
Left: View of carving on cloister pillar.
Right: View from northeast across garth.

Brú na Bóinne

County Meath

Map no. 97; GPS: N 53.694915, W 6.446443; Irish Grid: O 02668 72793

Brú na Bóinne or 'Palace of the Boyne' is the name given to an area within a bend of the River Boyne which contains a remarkable complex of Neolithic passage tombs, standing stones, and other prehistoric enclosures. The three major sites, Dowth, Knowth and Newgrange, dominate the area, though an additional ninety monuments have also been recorded, including forty similar, but much smaller, mounds. Construction of the tombs began around 3300 BC and they ceased to be used as burial sites in about 2900 BC, though the area was visited repeatedly during the Bronze Age, Iron Age, and Medieval periods. Newgrange, Knowth and Dowth were listed as National Monuments in 1882 and the Brú na Bóinne complex was listed as a UNESCO World Heritage Site in 1993. The complex is accessed by the Brú na Bóinne visitor centre, from where a shuttle bus transports visitors to the tombs at Newgrange and Knowth.

Knowth

The great mound at Knowth measures about 80m by 95m and rises to a height of about 12m. It is surrounded by a kerb of 127 stones, many of which are decorated with megalithic art. The mound contains two passage tombs, placed back to back, one facing east and the other west. The east-facing tomb has a 35m-long passage, leading to a cruciform-shaped chamber with a corbelled roof. The west-facing tomb has a 32m-long passage, leading to a rectangular chamber that is little more than a widening of the passage. Nineteen smaller satellite tombs surround the great mound, at least two of which were built before the great mound. Many of the tomb's interior structural stones are decorated with megalithic art, including spirals, lozenges and concentric circles. The Knowth site contains about half of the decorated stones in Brú na Bóinne and a quarter of all known megalithic art in Western Europe. Around AD 800, Knowth became a royal residence of the kingdom of North Brega and a large settlement grew around the mound, with many rectangular houses and souterrains constructed. In the late twelfth century, Anglo-Normans used the great mound as a motte, adding fortifications to its summit.

Dowth

The mound at Dowth measures about 90m in diameter and rises to a height of 15m. It is surrounded by a kerb of 115 stones, some of which are decorated with megalithic art. There are two passage tombs which face west, and both are closed off by gates. The most northerly of these tombs has a passage about 8m long, leading to a cruciform-shaped chamber decorated with megalithic art, with a large stone basin at its centre. The original

Above: View of south tomb entrance at Dowth.

Neolithic entrance has been disturbed by a souterrain, inserted in the early Christian period, and an access shaft built late in the nineteenth century. The southern tomb has a passage about 3m long, leading to a circular chamber. During midwinter, the setting sun aligns with this passage, illuminating the entire chamber. The crater in the centre of the mound is the result of excavations carried out in the 1840s. Prior to this, John Netterville, sixth Viscount Netterville, who resided in the nearby Dowth Castle, had erected a summerhouse on its summit.

Newgrange

The mound at Newgrange has a diameter of about 80m and rises to a height of about 13m. It is surrounded by a kerb of ninety-seven large rectangular boulders, placed horizontally end to end, many of which are decorated with megalithic art. The entrance stone, decorated with a triple spiral, and the stone opposite it on the north side of the mound, are the most notable of the decorated stones in Brú na Bóinne. The mound contains a single tomb, the passage of which is 19m long, and leads to a cruciform-shaped chamber measuring about 5m by 6m. It has a spectacular corbelled roof which rises to a height of 6m. The passage and chamber are richly decorated with megalithic art. The north and west recesses of the chamber contain single, large, stone carved basins, whilst the east recess contains two basins. Above the entrance to the tomb there is an aperture (roof-box), about 1m wide and 0.25m high, which aligns exactly with the rising sun on the morning of the winter solstice, and one or two days either side of it, so that at 8.58 a.m. (GMT) the chamber is illuminated for just seventeen minutes. Around the perimeter of the mound are the remains of the Great Circle, a stone circle thought to comprise originally about thirty-five stones, of which twelve remain.

View of the reconstructed quartz face and kerbstones.
(Note the standing stones, part of the Great Circle,
in the middle ground.)

Above: View of Newgrange from southeast.
Left: View of tomb entrance with roof-box above and decorated entrance stone in front.

Hill of Tara

County Meath

Map no. 98; GPS: N 53.580583, W 6.610379; Irish Grid: N 92089 59844

The Annals of the Four Masters and other ancient sources record this site as the chief residence of the High Kings of Ireland, from the time of Slainge, the first of the Firbolg kings, for a period of about 1,855 years. It saw the reign of 142 monarchs, the first 136 of whom were pagan and the last 6 Christian. The first of the Christian kings was converted by St Patrick who lit his paschal fire a few kilometres away at Slane, on the evening before Easter about AD 432. The last of the High Kings to reside at Tara, Diarmaid Mac Fergus Ceirbheoil, died in the year 565. A visit to Tara today may be somewhat disappointing as the only evidence of its royal occupation is a series of low-lying, grass-covered earthworks. There are about thirty visible monuments spread over the hill and a further thirty visible in aerial photographs and through geophysical survey. The earliest and most visible is *Duma na nGiall* or Mound of the Hostages, a Neolithic passage tomb, constructed around 3000 BC. Further to the south are two joined, ring-shaped earthworks, *Teach Cormaic*, or Cormac's House (a bivallate ringfort), and the *Forradh*, or Royal Seat (a ringbarrow). The 1.5m-high phallic stone, standing near the centre of the *Forradh*, is believed to be the *Lia Fáil* or

Stone of Destiny. It was used in the coronation ceremony and is said to have roared when touched by the rightful king. These monuments are within the limits of *Ráth na Rí* or the Kings' Fort. To the north of the Mound of the Hostages is the Mound of the Synods. It was devastated by a group of British Israelites between 1899 and 1902, who believing it contained the Ark of the Covenant, excavated it, finding just fifteen Roman coins. Further north is a long, rectangular feature known as the Banqueting Hall, which is probably a ceremonial avenue, and three circular earthworks known as *Claoinfhearta* or the Sloping Trenches and Gráinne's Fort (all ringbarrows).

Above: View from *Teach Cormaic* to *An Forradh*.
Left: View north along the 'Banqueting Hall'.

Kells Monastic Site

County Meath

Map no. 99; GPS: N 53.727547, W 6.880907; Irish Grid: N 73914 75885

It is thought the monastic settlement was founded here in AD 807 by monks who relocated from St Columba's (also known as Colmcille) community on Iona in western Scotland, because of constant attacks from Vikings. Over the following centuries Kells became a great school of learning and art and continued to flourish in spite of continued Viking raids. The monastery's greatest treasure, the Book of Kells, was stolen in 1007, but was returned, minus its cover, two months later. After dissolution, Kells Abbey became a parish church and the book continued to be kept there until about 1650, when the arrival of Cromwell's army prompted its dispatch to Dublin for safekeeping. By 1651, the book was in Trinity College where it has remained ever since. Today the physical presence of the monastery is evident throughout the town. The modern road layout follows the old monastic enclosure boundaries, so from the air the shape of the monastery can be determined. At the centre, within the inner enclosure, is the eighteenth-century St Columba's Church. Close to the church is the round tower which stands a little over 26m high. At its summit are five windows, each of which faced one of the five roads that entered Kells. Nearby is the South Cross, probably dating from the ninth century, it is dedicated to St Columba and St Patrick. To the northwest is the shaft of another cross and beside the church an unfinished high cross with a Crucifixion scene on one of its faces. Outside the church enclosure, a little to the north, is St Columba's House (more commonly known as St Colmcille's House), a stone oratory, possibly from the twelfth century. The Market Cross now stands beside the old Kells courthouse. It once stood at a busy crossroads, but was relocated here after an unfortunate accident involving a school bus in 1996.

Above: View of St Columba's House.
(Note: this entrance is a modern insertion.)
Left: View of the east face of the Market Cross.

Trim Castle

County Meath

Map no. 100; GPS: N 53.554357, W 6.789765; Irish Grid: N 80258 56708

In 1172, Hugh de Lacy, Lord of Meath, built a fortification on this site comprising a motte and timber tower. He left it in the hands of Hugh Tyrrell, who a year later set fire to the structure and fled when facing attack by Roderick O'Connor, King of Connacht. De Lacy later married Roderick's daughter and started to rebuild the fortification in stone. It was completed by his son, Walter, and became the largest Anglo-Norman fortress in Ireland. The massive central keep, with walls over 3m thick, is square in plan, with smaller square towers projecting from each of its sides. The outer curtain wall, two thirds of which still survives, was built on ground cut down to the bedrock. It contains two levels of arrow loops and is studded with towers and two main gatehouses. The west gate, facing the town and known as Trim Gate, is the earlier gateway and still serves as the main entrance. The Dublin Gate, on the south side, is a rare example with an external barbican tower. The future Henry V lived in this tower for a time as a boy around 1399. Both gates were protected by a drawbridge, portcullis and murder holes. The castle changed hands a number of times before passing to the Geneville family when Walter's granddaughter, Matilida, married Geoffrey de Geneville, and to the Mortimer family when Joanna de Geneville married Roger Mortimer. It appears the castle ceased to be a residence after the middle of the fourteenth century, although it was refortified during the Irish Confederate Wars, before falling to Cromwell's army in 1649. It later passed via the Encumbered Estates Court into the hands of the Dunsany Plunketts. Lord Dunsany sold the land and buildings to the Irish State in 1993, after which the OPW began a programme of conservation and opened the castle to the public in 2000. The castle was used in the making of Mel Gibson's film *Braveheart*.

Left: View of keep interior, looking downwards.
Top: Interior view of the Dublin Gate.
Above: View from top of keep over Dublin Gate and the curtain wall.

Clones High Cross

County Monaghan

Map no. 101; GPS: N 54.178951, W 7.232373; Irish Grid: H 50172 25820

A monastic settlement was founded at Clones by St Tighernach in the first part of the sixth century. Legend relates that the site was surrounded by water, from which the town of Clones derives its name, in Irish *Cluan Inis*, or Island of the Retreat. It is said the bell that hung in the island's abbey held sacred powers and at one time, when facing attack, the monks dispatched the bell to be conveyed to the mainland by boat for safekeeping. The enemy, however, was waiting for the monks on the shoreline and to prevent the bell falling into their foe's hands, they threw it into the lake. In the middle of the nineteenth century a man named Ned Drum was digging a trench and found the solid silver bell clapper. It was apparently quickly sold to a local silversmith and melted down. The rest of the bell was never recovered. The monastery's high cross now stands in the 'Diamond' (market place) of the town. Today it actually comprises the shaft of what is thought to be a ninth-century cross and the head of a different cross. On the west face of the shaft, the scenes leading upwards are: Adam and Eve depicted standing beneath the Tree of Knowledge, around which the serpent is twining; the Sacrifice of Isaac; and Daniel in the Lions' Den. On the east face are scenes of the Adoration of the Magi, the Marriage Feast at Cana and the Miracle of the Loaves and Fishes. The cross head depicts scenes of the Crucifixion.

Clones Round Tower and Shrine

County Monaghan

Map no. 102; GPS: N 54.178009, W 7.232802; Irish Grid: H 50145 25715

In a graveyard, a few hundred metres south of the high cross, is the 23m-high Clones round tower. It is thought to date from the ninth century and originally had five floors. The second, third and fourth floors are lit by small windows, facing in ascending order south, north and east. The fifth floor had four windows, facing the cardinal points. Much of the fifth floor is missing, as is the conical cap that probably once covered the tower. At its base the tower has a diameter of about 5m, with walls about 1.2m thick. The flat-headed tower doorway is about 1.6m above ground level. The interior was excavated in the middle of the nineteenth century, revealing a large quantity of human bones, including four skulls. Just east of the tower is an unusual house-shaped stone sarcophagus. It is carved from a single block of sandstone, probably as a copy of an earlier shrine made of metal and wood. It is thought to date from the twelfth century and probably once held the remains of St Tighernach. The sarcophagus was appropriated in the eighteenth century to cover a burial vault. It was subsequently the subject of some dispute between two rival families, the MacDonnells and the McMahons, with the result that its lid was inscribed and then deliberately defaced. Legend relates that underneath the sarcophagus is a large burial vault. The method of interment was that the coffin was lowered into the vault, where the corpse was removed and laid on a table next to the empty coffin. Quicklime was then applied. When the next corpse came any remains on the table were cleared and the procedure repeated.

Clonmacnoise Monastic Complex

County Offaly

Map no. 103; GPS: N 53.326349, W 7.98588; Irish Grid: N 00990 30650

In about 549, St Ciarán founded this monastic settlement at the point where the main land route running east–west through Ireland crossed the River Shannon. Ciarán died of the plague shortly after the site was established. His successor, Oenna, and the following abbots saw it become one of the best-known monasteries in the whole of Europe and an important urban centre. Some of the early known Irish manuscripts, including the eleventh-century Annals of Tighernach and the twelfth-century Book of the Dun Cow, were written here. The Cross of the Scriptures, the finest high cross in Ireland, was carved here in the tenth century. Peaceful monastic life was often disturbed by raiders and Clonmacnoise was plundered or burnt at least twenty-seven times by the Irish, seven times by Vikings and six times by Anglo-Normans. It fell into decline from the thirteenth century onwards until it was destroyed in 1552 by the English garrison from Athlone. Though designated a National Monument in 1882, Clonmacnoise continued to deteriorate until 1955, when it was placed it in the care of the Irish State. Today it is in the guardianship of the OPW. An interpretative centre houses numerous artefacts, including the north and south crosses and has the Cross of the Scriptures as its centrepiece. Outside, the eight ruined churches and two round towers have undergone comprehensive conservation works. They include the ninth- or tenth-century shrine chapel, Temple Ciarán and the twelfth-century Temple Finghin, a Romanesque church with a round tower attached that was involved in a landmark prosecution case when vandalised by a person from Birr in 1864. The cathedral, the largest structure on the site, was started by Flann mac Maeleachlainn, High King of Ireland, in 909 and was altered in the twelfth, thirteenth and fifteenth centuries.

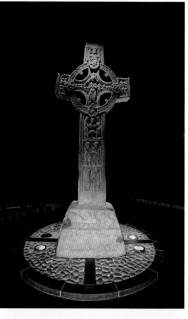

Left: View of round tower attached to Temple Finghin from north. **Top right:** View of the Cross of the Scriptures (now housed in nearby visitor centre). **Bottom right:** View of cathedral north door in the Perpendicular Gothic style with Saints Dominic, Patrick and Francis above.

Rahan Churches

County Offaly

Map no. 104; GPS: N 53.278841, W 7.612753; Irish Grid: N 25881 25432

St Carthach founded a monastery here in the sixth century. Blathmac, King of Meath, had him expelled in 636, after which he retired to Lismore, County Waterford. The next abbot of the monastery was Constantine. Constantine had joined the community as an anonymous lay brother, and was occupied with hand-grinding corn for the monks with a quernstone. He was later discovered to be a Scottish king, who had given up his throne and gone in search of a simple life. He was encouraged to study at the monastery and went on to become its abbot. He subsequently returned to Scotland and founded a number of churches, including Kirkconstantine and Govan Monastery, on the banks of the River Clyde. Rahan Monastery was refounded about 760 by Fidhairle Ua Suanaigh and it flourished until the twelfth century. About 1200, the monastery adopted the Rule of St Augustine, after which it fell into decline. The remains of two churches and a tower house can be found on the site today. The eastern half of the Church of Ireland church, which is still in use, is an early-twelfth-century Romanesque cruciform church though the transepts are now in ruin. A beautifully decorated round Romanesque window can be seen in its east gable and was probably originally located over a western doorway. The cruciform plan of this church is unique amongst early Irish stone churches. The nave of this church was added in 1732. Another church, further to the east, dates from the fifteenth or sixteenth century and incorporates parts of earlier churches, including a fine Romanesque window and doorway. The scant remains of a tower house can be found in the east corner of the nearby graveyard.

Above left: View of west end of larger church with fine round Romanesque window at top and modern insertion at bottom.
Above right: Exterior view of East church entrance (stonework probably reused from an earlier church).
Left: View of east church (with curious onlooker to right).

Boyle Abbey

County Roscommon

Map no. 105; GPS: N 53.973998, W 8.29707; Irish Grid: G 80555 02775

Boyle Abbey was founded by the Cistercian Order in 1161, a daughter house of Mellifont Abbey in County Louth. It closely follows the typical layout of most Cistercian monasteries. It was built next to the Boyle River, which could be used as a source of both power and water. A strong outer wall surrounds a cloister, with a cruciform church built on the north side so as not to shade the cloister. Although construction of the church started when the monks first arrived, it was not consecrated until 1218. It has both Romanesque and Gothic features and is regarded as the finest Cistercian church to survive in Ireland. The capitals are decorated with striking foliage patterns and animal and human figures. A series of buildings, including a refectory, kitchen and living quarters for the monks, ran along the other remaining sides of the cloister. The cloister has entirely disappeared and little remains of the other buildings, except the gatehouse. By the fifteenth century the importance of Boyle Abbey had declined and after the dissolution of the monasteries, in 1569, the abbey, its lands and possessions were handed over to Patrick Cusack of Gerrardston, County Meath. The abbey was leased to William Usher in 1595. It was besieged by Hugh O'Neill, and given to Sir John King in 1603, whereon it became known as Boyle Castle and was used as a military barracks. In 1897, the abbey ruins were described as being covered with the most luxuriant growth of ivy to be seen on any ruin in Ireland. Today the structure is well cared for by the OPW.

Left: View across cloister to church nave arches.
Below left: View through doorway in east range to gatehouse.
Below right: View through cloister doorway to nave.

Castlestrange Stone

County Roscommon

Map no. 106; GPS: N 53.585665, W 8.270988; Irish Grid: M 82102 59545

Castlestrange Stone can be found beside the driveway of the Castlestrange Demesne, southwest of Roscommon town, between Athleague and Fuerty. The stone was moved to its present location, as an ornament to Castlestrange House. Its original location was not recorded. Castlestrange House was destroyed by fire in 1916, after which its outbuildings were converted into a smaller dwelling house. The oval-shaped granite stone dates from the Iron Age period and measures about 90cm in height. It is inscribed with an elaborate design of unbroken spirals in the La Tène style. The use of the stone is not known; however, it is assumed to have served some religious or ritual purpose. Very few of these decorated stones have been found in Ireland. At the time of writing, one of the others, the Turoe Stone, located at the Turoe Farm, County Galway, was being prepared for relocation to the National Museum of Ireland.

McDermott's Castle

County Roscommon

Map no. 107; GPS: N 53.989505, W 8.232579; Irish Grid: G 84793 04485

McDermott's Castle stands on Castle Island in Lough Key. Tomaltach 'of the Rock' is credited with building the first stone castle on the site around the year 1200. The island became the headquarters of the McDermott clan, and their fortress a renowned centre of hospitality. It was said any person calling on them would receive food and shelter, no matter what his/her social standing. According to legend, when Una Bhan McDermott fell deeply in love with a member of a rival family, Thomas Laidir McCostello, her father confined her to Castle Island where she died of a broken heart. McCostello would secretly swim out every night to visit her grave. Finally the cold waters were the end of him and the two were reunited when his grave was placed next to hers. It is said two rose trees grew over their graves and became entwined in a lover's knot. In the seventeenth century, the King family acquired the land around Lough Key through the Cromwellian Settlement and in 1809 built Rockingham House, a mansion designed by English architect, John Nash, on the shoreline close to the island. In the 1830s Robert King, Viscount Lorton, rebuilt the castle as a folly. William Butler Yeats visited the island on 13 May 1890, and was so transfixed by it that he planned to turn the island into a place 'where a mystical order would retire for a while for contemplation'. His idea came to nothing.

View of castle from southwest.
Below left: Exterior view of castle entrance.
Below right: View of castle interior.

Roscommon Castle

County Roscommon

Map no. 108; GPS: N 53.635453, W 8.193226; Irish Grid: M 87267 65070

The construction of the castle began in 1269 under the instruction of Robert de Ufford, chief governor in Ireland for Henry III. It is a keepless castle, with a nearly rectangular courtyard and a D-shaped tower at each corner. The gatehouse is on the eastern side with a smaller western gate and drawbridge. Felim O'Connor's (see Roscommon Friary) son, Aedh, who had succeeded his father as King of Connacht, was an ardent opposer of the Anglo-Normans, and burnt the unfinished castle in 1270, 1271 and 1272. After Aedh's death in 1274, the pace of construction increased dramatically and the castle was eventually finished around 1278. It became the centre of Anglo-Norman power over a wide area of Ireland and one of the primary royal castles in Ireland until the middle of the fourteenth century. It was attacked repeatedly and eventually taken by the O'Connors, who then held the castle until it was surrendered to the Dublin government in 1569. In 1577, it was granted, along with 17,000 acres, to the English soldier and administrator Sir Nicholas Malby. Malby constructed a fortified house in the northern half of the courtyard. He also removed some of the 2.5m-deep outer moat, which once surrounded the castle, and built an extensive walled garden and a fish pond. A grand tree-lined avenue was also added, which led from the castle to Roscommon town. The castle was attacked by Red Hugh O'Donnell in 1596 and again in 1599. It was also a scene of strife during the Confederate Wars of the 1640s and was surrendered to a Cromwellian force in 1652. After the Williamite Wars of the 1690s the castle fell out of use.

Left: View of a castle stairway.
Above: Interior view of southwestern tower.

Roscommon Castle

Roscommon Friary

County Roscommon

Map no. 109; GPS: N 53.624784, W 8.191885; Irish Grid: M 87353 63882

The Dominican friary at Roscommon was founded by Felim O'Connor, King of Connacht, in the year 1253. The king was buried here in 1265. His effigy, one of only two royal effigies known to exist in Ireland, the other being in Corcomroe, County Clare (p. 50), has been placed on a later tomb, on the north side of the chancel. It shows him dressed in a long robe, carrying a sceptre. The front slab of the tomb features a fine carving of eight gallowglasses, elite mercenary warriors recruited from Scotland to assist the local chieftains in defending their territory. Each gallowglass is shown with a protective coat of chainmail and an open-face helmet known as a bascinet. The friary was partly destroyed by a fire in 1270 and also extensively damaged when struck by lightning on the evening of Christmas Day in 1308. The church, which originally consisted of one long aisle, had a north transept added in the fifteenth century. The original lancet windows in the east and west walls were also replaced with tracery windows about this time. After the dissolution of the monasteries, the abbey was leased to a number of individuals: Thomas le Strange of Castlestrange in 1573, Sir Nicholas Malby, Lord President of Connacht in 1577 and Viscount Valentia in 1615. It eventually fell into disuse and became a handy source for stone and building material for construction work going on in Roscommon town. The friary steeple fell in 1794, apparently when a gentleman was attempting to procure stonework for his house.

Above: View of friary from northeast.
Left: View of tomb with effigy of Felim O'Connor, King of Connacht.
Right: View from nave to east window. Though now destroyed it was once a very fine tracery window.

Ballinafad Castle

County Sligo

Map no. 110; GPS: N 54.026031, W 8.335834; Irish Grid: G 78039 08578

Ballinafad Castle was built in 1590 by Sir Richard Bingham, Governor of Connacht. It provided protection for the Red Earl's Road, a strategic route through the Curlew Mountains, which allowed access between south Connacht into north Connacht and west Ulster. The castle was garrisoned by a force of ten men, under the command of Captain John St Barbe. In 1595, it was attacked and partially destroyed by Red Hugh O'Donnell. It was attacked again during the rebellion of 1641. Crown forces continued to occupy the castle throughout the 1650s but by 1680, less than 100 years after its construction, it had fallen into disuse. Aghanagh graveyard, about 1km north of the castle, contains the grave of Captain St Barbe and also a 1659 memorial to Winifred Hughes, wife of Henry Hughes who was Governor of Ballinafad Castle. The castle structure comprises a central rectangular four-storey block, measuring about 6m by 4m, with circular towers measuring 5m in diameter at each corner. The walls of the towers survive to their original height, however, the northeast and southeast walls of the main block are missing. The castle's floors were made of timber and have long since disappeared, as has the wooden spiral staircase which was installed in the west tower. The first floor has a large plain fireplace in the centre of the southwest wall. At the second- and third-floor levels, each of the rooms in the towers has a fireplace and there are also many gun loops. Each tower has a small defensive machicolation and on two of the towers, tall plain chimney stacks rise well beyond the height of the walls. The OPW substantially repaired and stabilised the castle structure in about 1940.

Interior view of one tower
looking upwards.

Carrowkeel Passage Tomb Cemetery

County Sligo

Map no. 111; GPS: N 54.056667, W 8.379908; Irish Grid: G 75169 12003

The extensive Neolithic passage tomb cemetery at Carrowkeel is situated on an isolated hilltop, at an altitude of 300m, in the Bricklieve Mountains, about 30km southeast of Sligo town. About twenty cairns are scattered over the mountain side, and a group of about fifty round enclosures, located just to the east, is thought to be the remains of a village, probably once inhabited by the people who built the cairns. The majority of the cairns remained undisturbed until 1911, when fourteen were identified by letter and opened by excavation. One of the men involved, Robert Praeger, described entering one of the cairns in his 1937 book *The Way That I Went*: 'I lit three candles and stood awhile, to let my eyes accustom themselves to the dim light. There was everything, just as the last Bronze Age [*sic*] man had left it, three to four thousand years before.' Cairn G, one of the most impressive on the site, is about 7m high and 21m in diameter at its base. The entrance features a roof-box, similar to Newgrange, where, during the summer solstice, sunlight shines along the passage, brightly illuminating the interior. The main central chamber is about 1.5m in diameter, and is surrounded by three small cells each about

0.6m diameter, giving a cruciform shape to the plan of the structure. The 1911 excavation of the site revealed large quantities of human bones, representing at least sixty individuals, as well as cremated bone which filled many of the chambers to a depth of more than 7cm. Artefacts found included fragments of Carrowkeel ware, bone pins and pendants, stone balls and two intact Bronze Age vessels.

Above: Interior view of Cairn G.
Left: Interior view of Cairn H.

Carrowmore Cemetery

County Sligo

Map no. 112; GPS: N 54.250885, W 8.519468; Irish Grid: G 66188 33679

Carrowmore is amongst the largest and oldest megalithic cemeteries in Ireland. In the early 1800s the site was unscientifically excavated by a local landlord. Records were not kept and some of the artefacts discovered were sold to the Duke of Northumberland, who put them on display in his museum in the Postern Tower at Alnwick Castle in England. The first detailed survey of the site was undertaken in 1837 by George Petrie, during the completion of the first *Ordnance Survey of Britain and Ireland*, when fifty-eight monuments were mapped and numbered. In the 1880s another local landlord, William Wood-Martin, excavated twenty-two of the tombs. In the late 1970s and 1990s a Swedish archaeological team carried out extensive excavation campaigns. One of the tombs excavated, despite having been already explored by Wood-Martin, yielded 32kg of cremated bone. Radiocarbon dating of charcoal samples showed that the various tombs on the site were used mainly in the period 4000 BC to 3000 BC. Most of the monuments are boulder/dolmen circles – circles of stones with centrally placed polygonal chambers with capstones. The central tomb, numbered 51 and known as Listoghil, is the only tomb on the site that is covered by a cairn and probably dates to around 3600 BC. Before excavation, Listoghil was a sprawling uneven mound, about 2.5m high, with the capstone of the central chamber exposed. It had apparently served as a local stone quarry for many years. After excavation, it was restored to its original shape, with a new access passage and the chamber left exposed. Today the Carrowmore site is in care of the OPW. A small farmhouse has been converted into a fine visitors' centre and about thirty tombs are accessible, laid out in an oval pattern around Listoghil.

Top: View of Listoghil with Queen Maeve's tomb on Knocknarea in background. **Above:** View of chamber at centre of Listoghil.

Creevykeel Court Tomb

County Sligo

Map no. 113; GPS: N 54.435457, W 8.441706; Irish Grid: G 71386 54190

Creevykeel is one of the finest court tombs to be found in Ireland. In its present form it is termed a full court tomb but there is evidence that it was once a simpler monument with an open court. At least two episodes of alteration have been suggested. The cairn measures about 55m long and 25m wide at the broader eastern end. A 5m-long passage at the centre of the eastern end leads to an oval court 15m by 9m. The interior of the court is surrounded by a wall of upright stones with a façade of eight large stones at the western end. At the centre of this façade, a dramatic portal leads into a central double chamber, measuring about 9m by 3m, divided by a pair of jamb stones so that the first chamber is slightly larger than the second. The chambers were probably originally covered by a corbelled roof, forming an interior space more than 2m high. Further to the west, three smaller chambers all have separate entrances from the sides of the cairn. The Harvard Archaeological Expedition excavated Creevykeel in the summer of 1935. Amongst the discoveries were four carefully placed groups of cremated bone, two in each of the central chambers. Artefacts found included two polished stone axes, one placed at the entrance to the monument, and a second between the two central chambers. Hearths, pits and stake holes, as well as the keyhole-shaped structure in the forecourt are the remains of an early medieval metal-smelting operation. Local folklore relates that during the twentieth century the tomb was a favourite spot for hiding poteen stills. The illicit liquor was saved numerous times by a large white hare appearing on a stone wall beside the cairn, warning the poteen makers of the approach of the authorities.

Clockwise from top left: View of site from west. (Note three chambers with separate entrances.); View of central chambers from west; View of portal from within chamber; View of site from east.

Queen Maeve's Tomb

County Sligo

Map no. 114; GPS: N 54.258907, W 8.57337; Irish Grid: G 62682 34599

This massive Neolithic monument is located on the summit of Knocknarea Mountain, at a height of 327m above sea level. It measures about 60m in diameter at the base and rises in height to about 10m, forming a truncated cone with a flat platform. The weight of the stones that form the cairn is estimated to be at least 27,000 tons. Much of the stone used in its construction was quarried nearby and a massive hollow remains about 300m from the monument. There are five smaller monuments surrounding it. From the surrounding area it is one of the most stunning and highly visible locations of any Neolithic cairn, and from its summit there is a wide panoramic view for 40km in all directions. Legend relates that this is the final resting place of Queen Maeve of Connacht, the fierce warrior queen who reigned in the first century AD. She is supposedly buried standing upright, still in full armour, and facing her ancient foes in Ulster. Whether she was a true historical queen or a mythical character remains a matter of controversy. The cairn has never been excavated, but is thought to contain a Neolithic passage grave, probably with an inner chamber close to the centre of the cairn. According to local lore, people climbing the hilltop should bring a stone with them and add it to the mound in order to have a wish granted, and also to stop the queen from ever emerging from her tomb. The same lore relates that no good will ever come to those who remove stones from this ancient monument.

Above: View from cairn to southwest.
Left: View to cairn with small satellite tomb remains in foreground.
Below: View of site from west.

Sligo Friary

County Sligo

Map no. 115; GPS: N 54.270888, W 8.47018; Irish Grid: G 69416 35883

Sligo Friary was founded for the Dominicans in 1252 by Maurice Fitzgerald, the second Baron of Offaly. Fitzgerald also founded a Franciscan friary at Youghal, County Cork and had built Sligo Castle a few years earlier. The friary survived the ravages which destroyed Sligo town and castle in the thirteenth and fourteenth centuries, but was accidentally destroyed by fire in 1414. The Pope granted indulgences to all who contributed to its restoration, and two years later it was rebuilt by Friar Bryan MacDonogh. The friary church comprises a nave with an aisle and transept on the south side. The fifteenth-century rood screen between the nave and chancel, which separated the friars from the lay brothers, is a rare surviving example. The chancel, with its eight lancet windows in the southern wall, along with the sacristy and chapter house are the oldest parts of the friary, dating from its foundation. The high altar, the only sculptured example from a monastic setting in the country, the tower and the east window are fifteenth-century additions, as are the cloister and other domestic buildings found further to the north. The friary escaped suppression under the dissolution of the monasteries on condition that the friars were converted into

secular priests. In 1641, Sligo town was attacked and burned by Sir Frederick Hamilton. By this time, the friars had returned, and two of them were killed by Hamilton's soldiers, who then sacked and burnt the friary. The friars, however, continued in residence up until the 1760s, when they relocated to a nearby more modern dwelling. The Dominican order is still in Sligo town today. The friary lands eventually became the property of Lord Palmerston and, after his death, the friary was vested in the care of the Irish state in 1913.

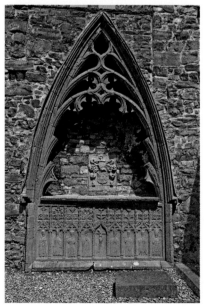  

Clockwise from top: View of friary from southeast; View of cloister walkway; View through rood screen to chancel; View of O'Crean tomb in north wall of nave.

Ahenny High Crosses

County Tipperary

Map no. 116; GPS: N 52.41276, W 7.393498; Irish Grid: S 41320 29151

The only remnants of the ancient monastic site of Kilclispeen are the two sandstone high crosses which stand in a graveyard at Ahenny. The crosses date from the eighth or ninth century, and are early examples of ringed high crosses. They are finely carved reproductions in stone of metalwork crosses. The bosses and cabled mouldings resemble the fixtures used to attach the metal sheets to wooden crosses and the carved decoration resembles that of metalwork. The cross to the north stands 3.7m tall and is the better preserved, despite the loss of a quarter of its ring. It is said that the missing stonework was broken away to make a stone for sharpening scythes and that the perpetrator 'had no luck after'. The cross to the south is a little shorter at 3.4m tall and the carvings, particularly around the base, are more worn. Both crosses carry almost every variety of Irish carving, with abstract geometric designs on the crosses themselves, and scenes featuring humans and animals on their bases. The scenes on the base of the north cross include: David bringing the head and body of Goliath to Jerusalem, a scene of Christ's Mission to the Apostles and Adam and the Animals. Both crosses have capstones, though that on the southern cross appears much eroded today. As at Killamery in County Kilkenny (p. 152), the capstones were used by locals to cure headaches by removing them from the crosses and placing them on the patient's head.

Left: View of east face of south cross.
Top: View of west face of north cross.
Above: Detail of carving on east face of north cross.

Carrick-on-Suir Castle

County Tipperary

Map no. 117; GPS: N 52.344975, W 7.408497; Irish Grid: S 40361 21600

The first castle was built here in 1309, on the site of a Poor Clare convent. It initially consisted of an enclosure, which gave protection to a section of the north bank of the River Suir. At this time, the town of Carrick-on-Suir was known as Carrick Mac Griffin, named after the Fitzgriffin family. In 1315, King Edward II made a grant of the manor to Edmund Butler, creating him Earl of Carrick and in 1328, his son, James, was created Earl of Ormond. About 1445, two tower houses, both five storeys high, were added, one at each side of the bawn. In about 1568, Thomas Butler, the tenth Earl of Ormond, added an Elizabethan manor house to the front of the structure. This house is unique in Ireland, being the only unfortified house of the period to survive reasonably intact. The house is two storeys, and U-shaped, forming a small inner court with the older structures at the rear. The interior is decorated with busts of the earl's cousin, Queen Elizabeth I, who was said to have promised to visit the house. Her promise, however, was never fulfilled. Other notable features of the house include the Long Gallery, over 30m in length, and the original A-framed oak truss roof. Carrick was the favourite house of the twelfth Earl, who became the Duke of Ormond. In 1670, he established a woollen industry in the town, which prospered for over a century. Later, however, the family deserted the house and it was let to various tenants. By the start of the twentieth century it was in a state of decay, with its grey walls covered in ivy and lichen. It increasingly fell into disrepair until it was placed in State care in 1947. Subsequently it has been restored by the OPW.

Above: View of castle from northeast.
Left: Interior view of tower house remains.
Right: View of inner court doorway.

Hore Abbey

County Tipperary

Map no. 118; GPS: N 52.519302, W 7.901831; Irish Grid: S 06714 40839

A Benedictine community was settled here at the end of the twelfth century. In 1272, after dreaming that the Benedictines were plotting to kill him, David McCarvill, the Archbishop of Cashel, removed the Benedictines and replaced them with Cistercian monks from Mellifont Abbey, County Louth. The archbishop was disliked by the Cashel town locals, particularly for his interference with their commerce. He introduced a levy of two flagons of beer from every brewing, which was collected from each of the thirty-eight local breweries. The layout of the abbey conforms to the typical Cistercian model; however, the cloister lies to the north, instead of the more usual south. This provided the monks with a better view of the Rock of Cashel but also meant the best sunlight would have been blocked by the church. The tower was added in the fifteenth century and late Gothic widows replaced the lancet windows in the east wall of the church. During the fifteenth century the church was reduced in size by blocking off half the nave and both transepts. The remainder of the nave was then converted for residential use, evidence of which can be seen in the blocked-up windows and arches and the remains of a fireplace. By the start of the sixteenth century the abbey had a community of just five monks. In 1540, following the dissolution of the monasteries, the abbey was surrendered by the last abbot, Patrick Stackboll. In 1561, Queen Elizabeth I granted the abbey lands to Sir Henry Radcliffe. It was later granted to James Butler, then Thomas Sinclair, before becoming the property of the Earl of Mount-Cashel. It is now in State ownership and in the care of the OPW.

View of fine rib-vaulted crossing tower.
(Note blocked lancet windows with later windows inserted.)

Kilcooly Abbey

County Tipperary

Map no. 119; GPS: N 52.673494, W 7.572885; Irish Grid: S 28942 58079

Kilcooly Cistercian Abbey was founded in 1182 by Dónal Mór O'Brien, King of Thomond, with monks from Jerpoint, County Kilkenny. The church was built in the early thirteenth century, initially with a nave and two aisles. In 1445, after the monastery was almost totally destroyed by a fire, a large amount of reconstruction took place. The church was rebuilt without aisles and a new north transept, entrance porch and tower were added. The fine east window contains particularly good flamboyant tracery and under it are the altar and the effigy tomb of Piers Fitz Oge Butler who died in 1526. Unfortunately, the effigy of the knight has suffered some damage and much of his face has been chipped off. The tomb is signed by the sculptor Rory O'Tunney, who also carved the tomb at Grangefertagh, County Kilkenny (p. 148). In the western supports of the tower are unusual and very finely carved niches where grooves for the wooden miserere seats remain. These seats were probably used by the abbot and his deputy. In the wall of the south transept is a magnificently carved doorway which leads to the sacristy. Above and around the doorway are carved scenes depicting the Crucifixion, St Christopher, and also an image of a mermaid holding a mirror, perhaps as a warning against vanity. The wall is also carved with the arms of the Butler family and the door may have led to a private Butler family chapel. Outside, the cloister path still remains with a large tree growing at the centre of the cloister garden. The other domestic buildings include the chapter room, refectory, kitchen and dormitory. The building nearby was an infirmary or guesthouse. A little to the north of the abbey stands a columbarium or pigeon house. Kilcooly was used in the making of John Boorman's film *Excalibur*.

Above: View of magnificently carved doorway in south transept.
Left: View of effigy tomb of Piers Fitz Oge Butler.
Right: View of abbey stairway.

Rock of Cashel

County Tipperary

Map no. 120; GPS: N 52.519772, W 7.890007; Irish Grid: S 07516 40892

Legend relates that Conall Corc, King of Munster, established a fortress here late in the fourth century and that it was here that St Patrick converted the King of Munster to the Christian faith in the fifth century. Cashel continued to be a royal centre until 1101, when Murtagh O'Brien granted the Rock to the Church. In 1127, Cormac MacCarthy, then King of Munster, began building Cormac's Chapel, said to be the most remarkable Romanesque church in Ireland. Its magnificent north door consists of five concentric arches and the stonework inside is highly decorated, with the chancel containing the only surviving Romanesque frescoes in Ireland. The 28m-high round tower also dates to the twelfth century. The cathedral, by far the largest structure on the site, was built in the thirteenth century, replacing an earlier, smaller structure. It pushes up against the tower and dwarfs the chapel between its south transept and choir. The choir was built first, about 1230, and the transepts, crossing and nave were added in the following decades, with the square tower added in the fourteenth century. The rectangular residential tower at the west end dates from the fifteenth century and was the work of Archbishop Richard O'Hedian, who also built the Hall of the Vicars Choral, now the site entrance and museum. Late in the fifteenth century, Gerald Fitzgerald, eighth Earl of Kildare, set the cathedral on fire, giving the reason that he thought his sworn enemy, Archbishop David Creaghe, was inside. The fire damage must have been minor as it continued to serve as a Church of Ireland cathedral until the middle of the eighteenth century. The cathedral and other buildings on the Rock were placed into State care in 1869 and the site now forms one of the most popular tourist attractions in Ireland.

Clockwise from top left: Carving on arch stop;
Interior view of Cormac's Chapel looking east through
the chancel arch; View of cathedral north transept
with top of round tower just visible; View from
nave to residential tower at rear.

Beaghmore Stone Circles

County Tyrone

Map no. 121; GPS: N 54.703102, W 6.936493; Irish Grid: H 68609 84415

The Beaghmore site was first discovered in the 1930s by turf cutters and recognised by the local amateur archaeologist George Barnett. Excavations from 1945 to 1949 and again in 1965 removed a thick layer of covering peat, to reveal 1,269 stones, arranged in seven stone circles and about ten stone rows. A number of small round cairns were also found, all of which had kerbs of small boulders and most of which contained traces of cremated bone. All but one of the stone circles occur in pairs and at least one stone alignment and cairn is associated with each pair and the single circle. The interior of the single circle is filled with small upright stones referred to by the excavation team as 'the dragon's teeth'. Most of the stones on the site are fairly small, measuring less than 0.5m high. One of the cairns had a neatly built central chamber in which was found a polished stone axe head. After the excavations of 1965, radiocarbon dating and pollen analysis were carried out, revealing that the area of the site was once mainly forest with human intervention appearing around 3800 BC when Neolithic farming resulted in deforestation, cereal crop planting and later animal grazing. The cairns were dated to 1800 to 800 BC, indicating that the main features of the site were probably built in the Bronze Age. The function of the site is not clear. Some

of the stone rows roughly align with the midsummer sunrise, whilst others do not indicate any solar or lunar event. Another suggestion is that the construction of the site was an attempt to halt the expansion of blanket bog and restore fertility to the area. Following excavation it was necessary to construct a system of drainage channels to stop the bog once again covering the site.

Top: View of single stone circle with 'the dragon's teeth'. **Left:** View of southeastern circles. **Right:** View along a stone row.

Castle Caulfield

County Tyrone

Map no. 122; GPS: N 54.506308, W 6.834784; Irish Grid: H 75529 62613

Sir Toby Caulfield was an English soldier who fought in Spain and later against Hugh O'Neill, Earl of Tyrone. After O'Neill's 1603 defeat at Kinsale, Caulfied was rewarded for his services with a grant of part of O'Neill's forfeited estate. During the Plantation of Ulster he received a further 1,000 acres at Ballydonnelly, previously home of the O'Donnelly family and Donnell O'Donnelly who had fought with O'Neill and was killed at the Battle of Kinsale. In 1614, Caulfield started building a castle at Ballydonnelly, renaming it Castle Caulfield. In 1619, when the castle, a three-storey, U-shaped, unfortified house, was complete, it was said to be the finest house in Ulster. It measured about 25m long and 9m wide and had walls about 1.5m thick. The mullioned windows were made of cut stone. In 1620, Sir Toby was created Lord Caulfield, Baron of Charlemont. His nephew, Sir William Caulfield, succeeded him as second Baron. The third Baron, also named Toby, was shot on the orders of Sir Phelim O'Neill, the leader of the 1641 Rebellion. Patrick O'Donnelly then captured Castle Caulfield, declaring that he had seized back his family property. The castle was partially burnt; however, the Caulfield family returned in the 1660s after the fifth Baron, William, had Phelim O'Neill apprehended and executed for the murder of his brother. In 1665, William was created Viscount Charlemont. The Caulfield family later built the Casino at Marino and Charlemont House on Parnell Square, Dublin, now home of the Hugh Lane Dublin City Gallery. Caulfield Castle fell out of use at the end of the seventeenth century and thereafter became a ruin. It was taken into State care and restored and stabilised by the Ministry of Finance in 1956.

Clockwise from top: View of castle interior; View of castle walls with cut stone mullioned windows; View through castle gatehouse; View through window to castle interior.

Creggandevesky Court Tomb

County Tyrone

Map no. 123; GPS: N 54.618878, W 7.001252; Irish Grid: H 64568 74978

This court tomb at Creggandevesky lay protected under a layer of peat until 1979, when a local farmer began removing topsoil as part of a land reclamation scheme. As the peat was removed, the upper edge of three stones was revealed. Excavations then carried out from 1979 to 1982 revealed a fine court tomb in a remarkable state of preservation. The trapezoidal cairn is about 18m long and tapers from 13m wide at the court entrance to about 6m at the rear. The court area has fine views over the nearby lough. It is U-shaped and measures about 6m across and 5m deep. At the time the tomb was built, the entrance, at the centre of the court, faced towards the rising point of the midwinter sunrise. A portal, with a massive lintel, leads into the gallery which consists of three chambers, decreasing in height from front to back. The excavation uncovered the cremated bones of twenty-one people. The bone was radiocarbon dated to around 3500 BC with a spread of about 100 years, which may well reflect the period over which the tomb was used. The second chamber contained a number of grave goods including shouldered and round-bottomed pottery sherds, arrowheads and scrapers, a flint javelin head, flint knives and a fine necklace of 112 stone beads. The rear chamber yielded a leaf-shaped flint arrowhead.

Roughan Castle

County Tyrone

Map no. 124; GPS: N 54.556087, W 6.728482; Irish Grid: H 82315 68273

In 1611, Andrew Stuart, the third Lord Stuart of Ochiltree, moved from Scotland to Ireland where he was granted 3,000 acres in County Tyrone. In 1618, his son, also called Andrew, built Roughan Castle. It stands three storeys high and comprises a central tower about 6m square, flanked by round 2.5m-diameter towers at each corner. Each of the towers has several gun loops to provide defence in case of attack. The castle entrance was by a door in the northwest tower, a typical Scottish influence. Just inside the door a spiral staircase ascended to the upper storeys, where the main living area of the family was on the first floor, as indicated by a large fireplace in the north wall. There is an unusual carving of a small head on a stone under the second-floor doorway leading into the tower at the southeast. When Andrew died, the castle was acquired by his brother John, and on John's death by the youngest brother, Robert. It is believed Robert's first wife was Catherine O'Neill, granddaughter of Hugh O'Neill, Earl of Tyrone. When the 1641 Rebellion took place, Robert was appointed an officer in the rebel forces by their leader, Phelim O'Neill. In 1653, Phelim sought refuge on the crannóg (artificial island) on Roughan Lough, just below the castle but knowledge of his hiding place was passed to the Crown forces and he was captured, transferred to Dublin and executed. Robert became a loyal servant of parliament and was somehow pardoned for having played any part in the rebellion.

Tullaghoge Fort

County Tyrone

Map no. 125; GPS: N 54.610193, W 6.723933; Irish Grid: H 82499 74301

The splendid hilltop enclosure of Tullaghoge commands wide views and is a distinctive landmark, visible from miles around. It is thought that the site was important from the earliest times, though when the earthworks were constructed is not known. It came into historical prominence in the eleventh century when it became the headquarters of the *Cenél nEógain* (later the O'Neills). It continued as an inauguration place after the O'Neills transferred their court to Dungannon. Tullaghoge was under the stewardship of the O'Hagans who lived at the fort and they, together with the O'Cahans, performed the inauguration ceremony, the 'making of an O'Neill'. The ceremony was carried out on the hill slope, where the initiate sat on a throne made of the *Leac na Rí*, or Stone of the Kings. After the Primate's Mass, the new O'Neill made a promise to rule by Brehon law and to give up the throne when he became too old or frail to rule. A white wand, a symbol of the purity of government, was waved over the new lord's head and a golden shoe was thrown over his head to indicate that he would continue in the footsteps of his ancestors. In 1595, Hugh O'Neill became the last of the O'Neills to be inaugurated at Tullaghoge. The *Leac na Rí* was smashed by the English Lord Deputy Mountjoy, as he advanced north against the O'Neills in 1602. Mountjoy later made peace with the O'Neills and signed the Treaty of Mellifont, where Hugh O'Neill gave up his Gaelic title, language and Brehon law and swore loyalty to the Crown. Peace lasted only a few years before Hugh O'Neill left Ireland in the 1607 Flight of the Earls. His lands were seized by the new Lord Deputy, Sir Arthur Chichester, and were subsequently colonised during the Plantation of Ulster.

Gaulstown Portal Tomb

County Waterford

Map no. 126; GPS: N 52.205924, W 7.210293; Irish Grid: S 54037 06256

Gaulstown Portal Tomb is located 8km southwest of Waterford city, at the foot of a steep north-facing slope known locally as *Cnoc an Chaillighe*, or 'The Hill of the Hag'. The tomb is recognised as one of the finest portal tombs in Ireland and its situation, in a small wooded glade, creates a scene of striking beauty. The huge capstone, which is estimated to weigh about 6 tons, measures 4.2m by 2.5m and about 1m thick. It rests on two portal stones and a backstone. There are two other sidestones and a sill stone. A concrete base has been added to support the stones, though this does not detract too much from their marvel. A cist with a large rectangular roofstone, which is located about 8m to the southwest, may have been covered with the same cairn as the tomb. George Du Noyer, who worked for the Geological Survey of Ireland, made sketches of the tomb in 1864. The sketches show the stones standing in the same position, though without the surrounding woodland.

Matthewstown Passage Tomb

County Waterford

Map no. 127; GPS: N 52.175892, W 7.227272; Irish Grid: S 52828 02730

Matthewstown Passage Tomb is located on an elevated, exposed ridge close to the village of Fenor. The tomb consists of five orthostats on each side, supporting three roofstones and a backstone. The passage is open to the east and is about 3.5m long. Four kerbstones at the west indicate that it may have been covered with a cairn about 10m in diameter. When Eugene O'Curry visited the site in the 1840s, he recorded in his *Ordnance Survey Letters of County Waterford*, that a row of standing stones originally surrounded the tomb. The early Ordnance Survey maps show the tomb as 'Giants Grave called *Leaba Thomais Mac Caba*', which translates from Irish as 'Thomas Mac Caba's Bed'. A limestone rock on Inishmaan in the Aran Islands also bears the same name.

Reginald's Tower

County Waterford

Map no. 128; GPS: N 52.260455, W 7.105483; Irish Grid: S 61128 12407

A Viking fortification, probably made of timber and earth, was first built on this site around AD 1003, apparently by Reginald the Dane. It was then rebuilt in stone during the twelfth or thirteenth century. The tower measures about 17m in height and has a diameter of about 13m. A spiral staircase ascends within the 3m-thick walls to a conical roof and wall-walk. In the twelfth century, Reginald Mac Gillemaire was held in the tower and is possibly the same man who was later executed by King Henry II for attempting to prevent his landing by stretching a chain across the estuary. According to Giraldus Cambrensis, shortly after Henry II's arrival, a frog was found in a grassy meadow near Waterford. Everybody was astonished at the sight of this frog as it was the first ever discovered in Ireland. The frog, which was thought to have been a stowaway on a ship in the English fleet, was brought before Sir Robert le Poer, Henry II's marshal, who lived in Reginald's Tower. The poor frog was solemnly interned in the tower, where it spent the rest of its days. A mint was established in the tower in 1185. It subsequently served as a royal castle and was visited by King John and Richard II. In 1463, the Irish Parliament also established a mint in the

tower. From 1663, it was used for the storage of military equipment and later as a general government storehouse. In 1819, it was converted for use as a prison with heavily barred cells installed on the ground floor. Later it became the residence of the Chief Constable of Waterford. In 1955 the tower was converted into a civic museum and opened to the public. Today it serves as a museum for Viking Waterford.

Left: View of descending castle stairway.
Top: Interior view of castle window.
Above: Interior view of first floor of castle.

The French Church

County Waterford

Map no. 129; GPS: N 52.260498, W 7.106979; Irish Grid: S 61025 12411

In 1240, Sir Hugh Purcell founded a monastery here for the Franciscan order. It was reformed by the Observants in 1521. At the time of the dissolution of the monasteries in 1539, it consisted of a church and steeple, a cemetery, a hall, six chambers, a kitchen, two stables, a bakehouse and four cellars. In 1545, Henry VIII granted a charter by which the nave and aisles became the Holy Ghost Hospital. In 1693, the chancel was given to the French Huguenot refugees to be used as a church, hence it became known as the French Church. The first minister, a Frenchman, Rev. David Gervais, was awarded a salary of £40 per annum. Services were held here until the death of the last minister, Rev. P. A. Franquefort in 1819. In 1746 the Holy Ghost Hospital was described as consisting of two great rooms which were occupied by twenty-four poor Catholic widows. The hospital was vacated in 1878 and by 1898 it was in ruins, with the roof structure collapsed onto the floor. By 1912 the whole building was roofless with around thirty grave slabs forming the pavement of the ruined church. The building was eventually taken over by the OPW and the grave slabs were realigned vertically along the walls in 1959.

Left: View from crossing tower to east window.
Top: Carving of rabbit wearing shoes under east window.
Above: Owl carving on corbel.

St Féichín's Church

County Westmeath

Map no. 130; GPS: N 53.681459, W 7.228703; Irish Grid: N 51014 70450

St Féichín founded a monastic settlement at Fore around the year 630. The community rapidly expanded and soon comprised 300 monks who were teaching more than 2,000 students. Although St Féichín's Church could date to the tenth century, according to legend it was constructed by St Féichín and his team of workmen. The story goes that the workmen struggled for some days to raise the doorway's lintel, a massive stone measuring about 1.8m long, 0.5m high and 1m thick. The highly venerated saint sent the workmen away and spent some time in holy prayer, after which he took the stone under his arm and quickly set it in place himself. The lintel has an unusual engraving of a simple cross within a circle. In the early thirteenth century a chancel was added to the rectangular church with *antae* and in the fifteenth century the east window was inserted. The arch which divides the chancel from the nave was rebuilt in 1934. It has a small carved head of a monk on its north side. Further up the hill is the Anchorite's Cell, in a fifteenth-century tower with a later chapel attached to the west. Anchorites took a vow of solitude and then lived the rest of their lives as hermits, never again leaving the confined space of their cell. One of the last anchorites to occupy it, Patrick Beglin, is said to have spent a portion of every day digging his grave in the oratory floor with his fingers. He carved his epitaph on stone in 1616 asking for prayers from future visitors.

Left: View from doorway to chancel arch and east window.
Right: Interior view of west door and large lintel.
Below: View of Anchorite's Cell tower with later chapel at right.

Fore Priory

County Westmeath

Map no. 131; GPS: N 53.683937, W 7.227201; Irish Grid: N 51110 70727

Hugh de Lacy founded the Benedictine priory of Fore in about 1180. The priory came under the authority of the Benedictine monastery of St Taurin's, in Normandy. It was colonised with French monks who collected tithes and returned any surplus revenue to the mother house in France. At the time of the priory's foundation, Normandy was still in the possession of the kings of England; however, that would later change. Subsequently any monastery with a French mother house was declared alien. During the Hundred Years' War all alien property was seized by the English Crown and, in exchange for an annual fee paid to the government, custody was returned to the prior. This system was open to corruption and government clerks and sometimes the priors lined their own pockets. In the early fifteenth century, Fore found itself outside the 'land of peace' and often subjected to raids by the O'Reilly and O'Farrell clans. William Anglond, prior in 1417, started to fortify the priory and his successor, William Crose, continued enhancing its defence. The results of which we can see today in the two fifteenth-century fortified towers, one at the west end of the thirteenth-century church, and a second built over the sacristy on the south side of the church. The cloister, the remains of which were rebuilt in 1912, also dates from the fifteenth century. Fore was seen by the government as an outpost of the Pale and an important strategic point. This resulted in building of town defences, the gates of which can still be seen nearby. The last prior was William Nugent, the son of Richard Nugent, Baron of Delvin, to whom he surrendered the priory in November 1539, following the dissolution of the monasteries, when it was populated by just three: William, and the two monks, Walter Deece and Richard Herford.

Clockwise from top left: View to nearby town gates; View of cloister remains; View from nave to east window; View of garth to tower built over the sacristy.

Taghmon Church

County Westmeath

Map no. 132; GPS: N 53.601342, W 7.266769; Irish Grid: N 48591 61506

Taghmon Church was built in the fifteenth century, on the site of an earlier church associated with St Munna. Its structure is a little skewed, with the walls not quite meeting at right angles. The heavy stone vault which covers the church places considerable force on the side walls. Collapse of the structure was prevented in 1928, with the installation of tie bars which hold the side walls together. It is lit by four single-light ogee-headed windows at ground-floor level and a modern east window. An unusual piscina with an elaborately carved arch is found in the southern wall. There is an adjoining four-storey accommodation tower at the west end, entered through the church. The ground floor and third floor are vaulted and the upper levels are reached by a spiral staircase which continues to the roof. By 1587, the church was in possession of the Nugent family who resided nearby at Taghmon Castle. Legend tells that Cromwell slept one night in the church before laying the castle to ruin. In 1755, the church is recorded with its roof cracked from end to end, letting in the rain and everything inside in a very sorry order. The curate, Christopher Dixon, was described as a weak man who could not be trusted with money. He was given an allowance of £20 a year from the Bishop of Meath. This was supplemented with fees charged for his services of baptisms, weddings and funerals. Dixon would look down on his parishioners from his tower, and lower a basket at the end of a rope, in which monies would be deposited. It would be repeatedly lowered until Dixon deemed the payment sufficient for his services. The church was repaired in 1847 and again in 1928.

View of church interior looking towards east window.

Hill of Uisneach, 'centre' of Ireland

County Westmeath

Map no. 133; GPS: N 53.49208, W 7.554817; Irish Grid: N 29598 49187

The Hill of Uisneach rises to a height of 180m above sea level. On a clear day, from its summit, panoramic views stretch out over a plain with the hills and mountains of twenty counties visible on the distant horizon. The site has been identified as an important ceremonial and royal site, ranking in importance among locations such as Tara. Legend relates that it is the *Umbilicus Hiberniae*, *Axis Mundi*, or 'Navel of Ireland', where the five *cóiceda* or ancient provinces of Leinster, Munster, Connacht, Ulster, and *Mide* met. Traditionally, the exact spot where the provinces met is marked by the over 4m-high *Ail na Mireann* (Stone of Divisions) or Catstone, so named because it is said to have the appearance of cat watching a mouse. In folk tradition great bonfires were lit on the hill at Bealtaine (the beginning of May) for ritual purification. Excavations carried out between 1925 and 1930 revealed an extensive area of very intense burning and animal bones, some representing whole carcasses, which seem to confirm this

tradition. Survey and excavation have revealed a complex of earth monuments covering an area of about 2km square, including enclosures and barrows, two ancient roads and a megalithic tomb. The 1925–30 excavations concentrated on the largest monument, the figure-of-eight-shaped earthwork. Modern reinterpretation of the excavation shows that a late prehistoric ceremonial enclosure existed under the early medieval conjoined ringfort. The megalithic tomb, known as St Patrick's Bed, on the western summit of the hill, was, according to John O'Donovan who visited the hill in 1837 as part of his work for the first Ordnance Survey, 'much more perfect before the sappers removed the stones from it to form a trigonometrical station'. Today the remains of the tomb are overgrown and barely recognisable.

View of *Ail na Mireann* (Stone of Divisions).

Dunbrody Abbey

County Wexford

Map no. 134; GPS: N 52.283545, W 6.959174; Irish Grid: S 71081 15110

Dunbrody Abbey was founded *c.* 1178 by Hervey de Montmorency, marshal to Henry II and uncle of Strongbow. Montmorency assigned the land to the Cistercian abbey of Bildewas in Shropshire, but a lay brother, who was sent from Bildewas to survey the lands, reported back that it was a howling wilderness (owing to war) and in order to take refuge from the weather he had been obliged to live in the trunk of an old oak tree. Consequently the Abbot of Bildewas devolved his responsibilities to St Mary's Abbey in Dublin. The enormous early Gothic church was built in the early thirteenth century. The nave, aisles, chancel and transepts survive complete, except for the south arcade of the nave and aisle which have been reduced to their foundations. Each transept has three rib-vaulted chapels on the east side. Stairs in the south transept once led to dormitories, but these do not survive. The two-storey central fortified tower was added in the fifteenth century. Dunbrody was officially suppressed in 1536 and was soon after plundered and made unfit for the monks to return. In 1545, Sir Osborne Etchingham, marshal of the English army in Ireland, was granted the Dunbrody estate, and the south transept was converted into a mansion

house. Dunbrody passed to the Chichester family in 1642, when the heiress, Jane Etchingham, married Sir Arthur Chichester, Earl of Donegal. The abbey subsequently fell into disuse and on Christmas Eve 1852 a massive collapse occurred during a violent storm. The abbey interior was later recorded as being used to grow potatoes, whilst another part was used as a cow house. The Chichester family handed the abbey over to the OPW in 1911.

Opposite page: (left) View from abbey entrance. (Note blocked pointed arch to south aisle of nave.); (right) View from nave to crossing tower and east window.
Above: View of abbey from southeast.
Left: View from south transept to crossing tower and beyond.

Ferns Abbey

County Wexford

Map no. 135; GPS: N 52.589583, W 6.491697; Irish Grid: T 02271 49724

A Christian settlement was founded at Ferns in AD 598 by St Aidan. Vikings plundered the site in 834, 836, 839, 842, 917, 920, 928, 930 and finally in 937 when it was partly destroyed by fire. Dermot MacMurrough, King of Leinster, refounded the abbey as a house of Augustinian canons in 1158 'for the health of my soul and my ancestors and successors'. Its foundation charter included an entitlement to a portion of all beer brewed in Ferns. MacMurrough took sanctuary in the abbey whilst awaiting the arrival of his Anglo-Norman allies, later marching on Wexford, Waterford and then Dublin. He died in 1171, and, at his own request, was buried in the abbey grounds. Under the dissolution of the monasteries, the abbey was suppressed in April 1539 and the property with 630 acres of land reverted to the King of England. The remains of the abbey today include the north wall of the nave and chancel. Part of the barrel vault over the chancel survives and to the north, the sacristy and sacristan's room can be seen overhead. An unusual tower at the west end of the nave is square at its base and round from about halfway up. Inside the tower a narrow winding staircase leads upwards. The abbey cloister measured about 20m square, however, visible evidence of it does not remain. In the nearby churchyard the scant remains of an ancient stone cross are said to mark the grave of Dermot MacMurrough, King of Leinster.

Clockwise from top: View of church interior looking towards east window; View of tower doorway; View of cross base, said to mark the grave of Dermot MacMurrough; View of church interior looking towards east window.

Ferns Castle

County Wexford

Map no. 136; GPS: N 52.590737, W 6.499325; Irish Grid: T 01752 49842

Dermot MacMurrough, King of Leinster, erected an early structure on the site of the castle and it was here that, in 1152, he brought Dervorgilla, the abducted wife of Tiernan O'Rourke, King of Breifne. O'Rourke recovered his wife one year later, and the subsequent hostilities led MacMurrough to ally with the Anglo-Normans and their colonisation of Ireland. Giraldus Cambrensis recorded the building of a castle at Ferns by his Fitzgerald cousins at the end of the twelfth century. The castle was believed to have been completed by Earl William Marshall in about 1224. In 1299, Philip de Barry was the first recorded constable of the castle. In 1324 it was stated to be in need of repair. The castle became the residence of the Bishops of Ferns, but was captured by the O'Tooles in 1331, retaken by Bishop John Esmond, captured again by the Irish and retaken once more by Bishop William Carnells. In 1558, Richard Butler, Viscount Mountgarret, became constable of the castle. Subsequently Sir Thomas Masterson commanded an English garrison from the castle and his family held it until it was surrendered to Cromwell's general, Sir Charles Coote, in 1641. To prevent recapture the castle was then demolished. Excavations from 1972–1975 found evidence of a drawbridge and mostly late-thirteenth- and early-fourteenth-century pottery including the earliest dateable finds, which were French pottery (Saintonge ware) dated to 1280–1310. The castle originally consisted of a three-storey square keep with thirteenth-century trefoil-headed windows and a round tower at each angle. It was surrounded by a defensive fosse cut into the bedrock. Today, just the south and east walls of the keep survive. One tower remains intact and contains a fine Gothic chapel. A second tower survives only in fragments.

Clockwise from left: View of the Gothic chapel; View of tower interior; View from top of tower; View of surviving tower and walls at southeast.

Rathmacknee Castle

County Wexford

Map no. 137; GPS: N 52.269313, W 6.490688; Irish Grid: T 03084 14089

Rathmacknee Castle was built by a member of the Rosseter family, probably John Rosseter, in the middle of the fifteenth century. The Rosseters arrived in Ireland with the Anglo-Norman invaders and settled in the Barony of Forth with Rathmacknee as their headquarters. John Rosseter was made high steward of Wexford in 1451. The Rosseters built a number of structures on the site, with Rathmacknee Castle being their final stronghold. The castle consists of a tower house with an attached bawn, typical, though the best preserved, of a number of other castles in south Wexford. The five-storey tower, which is about 8m square, fills the southeastern corner of the bawn and is complete except for floors and roof. A low doorway in the west wall leads to a small lobby and at the left a steep mural stone staircase leads upwards. Each floor contains only one room. The second floor has a good fireplace and garderobe; the third floor has window seats and also a fireplace; the fourth floor, the uppermost room, has three small square-headed windows, all with window seats, but is without a fireplace. A wall-walk, at the base of the parapet walls, goes all around the roof and passes through turrets at the southeast and southwest.

The bawn walls are about 1.2m thick and 8m high with a well-preserved bartizan at the northeast corner. Thomas Rosseter took part in the siege of Duncannon Fort in 1643 and when this evidence was used against him by Cromwell's Commissioners, he forfeited all his Wexford estates and found himself transplanted to 66 acres of barren land in Connacht. He later drowned whilst on a voyage to France. A farmhouse, which is still occupied today, was subsequently built inside the Rathmacknee bawn.

Left: View of castle from south.
Top: View of defensive walls with bartizan at the northeast corner.
Above: View of castle windows.

Tacumshane Windmill

County Wexford

Map no. 138; GPS: N 52.208784, W 6.423998; Irish Grid: T 07783 07451

Tacumshane Windmill was built by the millwright Nicholas Moran in 1846. Virtually all of the timber used in its construction was driftwood or timber from shipwrecks. The windmill is three storeys high with a thatched roof. It was re-thatched in 1908 and in use until 1936, making it the last commercially working windmill in the Republic of Ireland. The power from the sails was transferred through massive gearing on the top floor to drive a vertical shaft to the floors below. Underdrift gearing drove two pairs of millstones on the first floor. A hoist, also driven by the sails, allowed sacks to be lifted between the floors. Outside the windmill, a tail pole and wheel allowed the sails, along with all the associated gearing in the top floor, to be directed to face the wind. The windmill was the first industrial archaeological monument to be taken into State care in the Republic of Ireland and it was restored as a working National Monument by the OPW in 1952. Though most of the mechanism remains in good order the windmill is no longer operational.

Clockwise from top left:
View of massive gear wheel
on the top floor;
View of wooden gear wheels;
Detail of gear teeth.

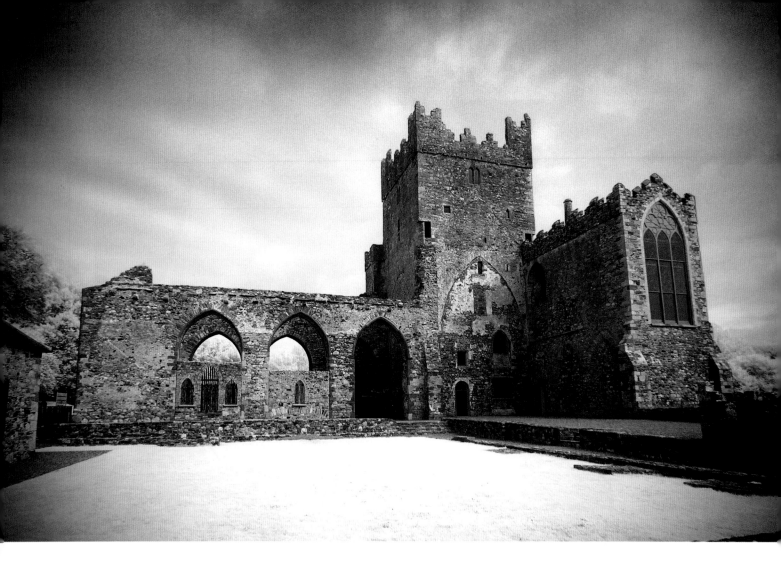

Tintern Abbey

County Wexford

Map no. 139; GPS: N 52.236953, W 6.837777; Irish Grid: S 79448 10052

The story of Tintern Abbey starts in the autumn of 1200 when, during a fierce storm off the south coast of Ireland, William Marshal, Earl of Pembroke and Lord of Leinster, vowed to found an abbey wherever he found the safety of dry land. On reaching Bannow Bay he granted 3,600 acres of land for the foundation of a Cistercian abbey which was colonised by monks from Tintern Abbey in Monmouthshire, Wales. Consequently Tintern is sometimes called *Tintern de Voto* or 'Tintern of the vow'. It became the third richest Cistercian abbey in Ireland. Following the dissolution of the monasteries, the abbey and its lands came into the hands of Anthony Colclough. He converted the tower and chancel into a fortified residence. In the early nineteenth century the nave was converted into a Georgian-Gothic mansion. A thriving weaving industry developed in Tintern village and, in the 1790s, John Colclough established a flour mill just southwest of the abbey. It is still visible, along with a walled garden, in the nearby wooded area. John died in a duel in 1807 and his brother Caesar continued John's plan to move tenants from Tintern village, to make way for gardens, to the new village of Saltmills. The Colclough family remained in residence until 1959 when Lucy Marie Biddulph Colclough left; the site was taken into State care shortly afterwards.

The thirteenth-century church, which underwent alterations in the fifteenth century, was originally cruciform in plan but only the centre aisle of the nave, the tower, chancel and Lady Chapel in the south transept, remain standing. The only claustral building to survive above ground is the gateway incorporated into the later stable block. Excavations carried out in the 1980s and 1990s revealed the cloister and abbot's seat. Most of the Colclough residence was removed at that time.

Left: View looking upwards into the crossing tower.
Top: Interior view of the Colclough family library above the Lady Chapel.
Above: View of tower interior.

Aghowle Church

County Wicklow

Map no. 140; GPS: N 52.767877, W 6.6204; Irish Grid: S 93169 69390

A monastic settlement was founded here by St Finnian in the early sixth century. The name Aghowle is derived from the Irish *Achadh Abhal*, or Field of the Apple Tree and the *Life of St Finnian* relates that an apple tree once stood here. Nothing remains of this early settlement. The large ruined single-celled church on the site today was built around the middle of the twelfth century. It measures about 18m long and a little over 7m wide. The gables and north walls survive to their full height, but the south wall is almost entirely missing. The dividing wall at the west end of the church is an eighteenth-century addition, built to form a burial vault for the Nixon family. The very fine granite carved west door is flat-headed and has a Romanesque double architrave moulding on the outside and a round arch on the inside. The drawbar hole inside the doorway is unusual for a twelfth-century church. There are two Romanesque windows in the east gable, below which are an ambry at one side and a shelf which probably contained a piscina on the other. The stone built into the wall below the shelf is most likely the base of the piscina as indicated by the drain hole passing through it. Just northwest of the church is an unfinished granite cross, over 3m in height and thought to date from around the year 1000. The large granite basin below the cross is said always to contain rainwater, every drop of which retains the blessing of St Finnian, and is able to effect many cures.

Left: View of unfinished cross and basin, the water of which is said to be blessed by St Finnian.
Right: View of ambry in east wall.
Below: View of east wall and Romanesque windows.

COUNTY WICKLOW: AGHOWLE CHURCH   293

Baltinglass Abbey

County Wicklow

Map no. 141; GPS: N 52.943738, W 6.710225; Irish Grid: S 86755 88847

Dermot MacMurrough, King of Leinster, founded a Cistercian monastery at Baltinglass in 1148. It was named *De Valle Salutis*, or 'The Valley of Salvation' and was colonised by monks from Mellifont Abbey in County Louth. In 1185, the abbot at that time, Albin O'Mulloy, spoke out against the English and Welsh clergy, criticising their evil ways and citing them as a bad example for the innocent Irish. In 1227, Abbot Malachy was removed from office and Baltinglass came under the authority of Furness Abbey in Cumbria, England. A new Anglo-Norman abbot was installed, of whom the community strongly disapproved. Legend has it he was driven out of the abbey, knocked off his horse and robbed of his monastic seal. It took an armed force to get him reinstated and after an investigation the monastery bursar was held accountable for the incident and expelled for a period of one year. In 1228, the community at Baltinglass comprised thirty-six monks and fifty lay brothers. In the Late Middle Ages, one of the abbots built a tower house just south of the abbey. This was demolished in 1882, in order to provide building materials for the nearby Church of Ireland church and rectory. Baltinglass was suppressed in 1536 and the chancel was subsequently adapted as a Protestant church. Today, the only surviving remains of the monastery are sections of the church and the adjacent small section of rebuilt cloister. The original church had a long-aisled nave and transepts. The impressive southern nave arcade survives with alternating round and square pillars, the capitals of which are decorated with unusual designs. There is a well-preserved sedilia in the presbytery. A later medieval crossing tower was inserted but was replaced in 1815 with a neo-Gothic style tower. The three lancet west windows are original twelfth century, but the three east windows date from the nineteenth-century rebuilding.

Opposite page: View of nave with west door at rear. **Clockwise from top:** View of abbey interior from west door; View of sedilia in chancel south wall; View inside nineteenth-century tower.

Glendalough Monastic Site

County Wicklow

Map no. 142; GPS: N 53.010529, W 6.327213; Irish Grid: T 12328 96811

St Kevin founded a monastic settlement at Glendalough in the sixth century. It is said that the saint first discovered the location whilst searching for an isolated retreat. He lived for many days by the Upper Lake, taking shelter in a hollow tree and sustaining himself with a meagre diet of wild fruit. Eventually, after falling into poor health, he was carried out by local herdsmen. He returned later with a community of monks and settled, according to the *Lives of St Kevin,* at the lower part of the valley where two clear rivers flow together. Today, this location is known as the Monastic City, and is the area occupied by the majority of the Glendalough ruins. Once the monastery was established, St Kevin again resumed the life of a hermit by the Upper Lake where, legend relates, he reached the impressive age of 120 years. Glendalough remained a prestigious centre of religious learning for the next six centuries, though surviving records contain little more than the deaths of numerous abbots as well as details of many disastrous fires and occasions of pillage. The first recorded destruction by fire was in the year 770, and over the subsequent four centuries the community was evidently destroyed twenty times. Vikings are blamed nine times, Irish once, accidental fire for three, another six are not specified, and in 1176, just after the arrival of the

Anglo-Normans, Glendalough was plundered by English adventurers. One year later, the community was hit with a disastrous flood, which swept away a bridge and a number of mills. Today the remains of the settlement include a number of churches of various dates and styles including, *Teampall-na-Skellig*, Reefert Church, St Mary's Church, The Cathedral (the largest church), St Kevin's Church (stone roofed with a small round tower), Trinity Church and St Saviour's Priory (best Romanesque decoration), as well as the 30m-high round tower and a number of crosses and other monuments.

Above left: View of St Saviour's Priory chancel.
Above right: View of graveyard, looking up the valley.
Left: View of cathedral interior looking east through chancel arch to east window.

Rathgall Hill Fort

County Wicklow

Map no. 143; GPS: N 52.802294, W 6.663165; Irish Grid: S 90212 73165

About 6km east of Tullow, located on a low rounded hill with an extensive view over the surrounding landscape, Rathgall hill fort is one of the largest in Ireland. It consists of four roughly concentric ramparts, enclosing an area of about 18 acres. The three outer ramparts, constructed from earth and stone, are thought to date from the Middle to Late Bronze Age, around 1400 to 1000 BC. The inner rampart was built of drystone, comprising small granite blocks, at a much later date, probably in the early medieval period. It varies in width, with an average height of about 1.5m and encloses an inner area about 45m in diameter. The site was excavated a number of times between 1969 and 1979. These excavations revealed a 35m-diameter circular enclosure with an external bank within the inner stone rampart. At its centre had been a circular, 15m-diameter wooden structure, probably an open-air palisaded enclosure. Near the centre was a cremation burial, in which was found a penannular gold ring, dating to 1290–1040 BC. The excavations also yielded numerous artefacts, including eighty-eight glass beads, one of the largest collections of such beads ever found in Europe. Just to the east, clay moulds used for casting high-status objects such as bronze swords, spearheads and rapiers were found in a workshop area. Rathgall was a prestigious site of major importance with evidence for use up to the post-medieval period. Its most intensive period of occupation was in the Middle to Late Bronze Age.

View of fort entrance.

Glossary

Ambry or aumbry: A recess in a church which vessels were stored.

Anglo-Irish: A term used to identify the privileged, generally Anglican, ruling class of Ireland from the late seventeenth century to the early twentieth. Many were descended from the new settlers who arrived with and after the Plantations.

Anglo-Norman: A term generally used to identify the settlers who arrived with or after the Norman invasion of 1169/1170. Generally thought of as Anglo-Norman, they were a mixed people, some of Norman descent who were born in England and Wales and others Flemish, etc. Other terms such as Anglo-French and Cambro-Norman are also used.

Antae (anta singular): Projections of the north and south walls of a church past the east and west walls with no practical function in a stone church but thought to copy a feature in older wooden churches.

Arcade: A range of arches carried on piers or columns either free-standing or attached to a wall.

Backstone: The lower stone opposite the entrance of a portal tomb on which the lower end of capstone rests.

Barrel vault: A semicircular arched roof.

Bartizan: A small turret projecting from the angle of two walls, e.g. on the top of a tower.

Battlement or crenellation: A parapet with alternating raised sections for protection. In Ireland often stepped.

Bawn: A walled enclosure attached to a castle, tower house, etc.

Cairn: A mound of stones.

Capstone: Flat roofstones in megalithic tomb, often enormous in portal tombs.

Chancel: The east end of the church where the main altar is located; usually applied to the area east of the crossing where it exists. In simple churches the narrow eastern end where the altar was located.

Choir: Part of the chancel reserved for choir and clergy.

Corbel: A projecting stone.

Corbelled roof: Roof built by placing each row of stones slightly projecting inwards beyond the course below, until the sides meet at the top.

Crossing: In a church the interception of the nave, chancel and transepts. Often the location of a crossing tower.

Curtain walls: The defensive walls of a castle, often with towers.

Dissolution of the Monasteries: The disbanding of religious houses by Henry VIII and his successors from 1536.

Flanking towers: Towers built to provide defensive positions on curtain walls.

Gallery: A passage in a megalithic tomb. It can be divided into chambers.

Gallowglass: Scots-Irish mercenary.

Gothic architecture: A style using pointed arches and introduced into Ireland by the Anglo-Normans. It can be divided into Early English, Decorated and Perpendicular.

Groin vault: Intersection of two barrel vaults at right angles.

Inhumation: The practice of burying corpses as opposed to cremations.

Insular style: A blending of Iron Age curvilinear ornament and Classical styles with Germanic and Anglo-Saxon animal ornament to produce what people know as the typical Irish style. It reached its zenith in the eighth century and continued with Viking influence into the twelfth century.

Lancet window: A tall, narrow window.

Lights: Openings between mullions of a window.

Machicolation: An opening in the floor of a parapet or turret.

Mullion: An upright post dividing a window.

Mural passage: A passage built within the wall of a structure, usually a church or castle.

Musket holes/gun loops: Small, circular openings in walls through which small firearms could be discharged.

Nave: The western part of a church; where a crossing exists, the area west of it. In simple churches the wider western end of the church.

Nave-and-chancel church: A simple church with a narrower eastern end where the altar was located often reached through a chancel arch.

Ogee-headed window: A Gothic window with an elegantly 'S'-curved, pointed head.

Old English: A general term to identify people of Anglo-Norman descent who by the seventeenth century had adopted many Irish customs and remained Catholic. The term Hiberno-Norman is also used.

Orders: A series of concentric arches receding towards the opening of a door or window; often used in Romanesque-style doorways.

Orthostats: Large stones set upright, especially in megalithic tomb.

Palisade: A wooden fence, often on top of a bank.

Parapet: A low wall around the top of a building or bridge; sometimes battlemented.

Pilaster: A shallow pier projecting from a wall.

Piscina: A stone basin set into the wall with a drain in the base used for washing communion vessels.

Portal stone: A large stone in a megalithic tomb forming one side of the entrance.

Presbytery: Area of the church east of the choir where the high altar is.

Respond: A half pier (a masonry support similar to a column but need not be cylindrical) attached to the wall and carrying one end of an arch.

Rib vault: A framework of diagonal arched ribs which allows lighter material to be used to fill the cells between.

Romanesque architecture: A style using round arches that developed into Hiberno-Romanesque in Ireland.

Rood screen: A screen dividing the chancel from the nave, set below the rood or crucifix.

Sedilia: Seats for clergy, often set into the chancel wall.

Septal stone: A stone slab separating compartments in a burial chamber.

Sill stone: A low stone dividing a gallery or compartments in a burial chamber.

Springer: The part of the wall where an arch starts.

Tracery: Ornamental intersecting pattern at the top of Gothic windows or openings. The most common type in Ireland was 'switch-line tracery'. Other forms include 'reticulated' which resembles an open net and 'flamboyant' which is flowing and flame-like.

Transept: North and south arms of a church, usually at the crossing.

Trefoil-headed window: A window with an arch reminiscent of a clover leaf.

Bibliography

BOOKS

Archdall, M., *Monasticon Hibernicum* (Dublin, 1876)

Barry, T. B., *The Archaeology of Medieval Ireland* (London, Routledge, 1988)

Bartlett, W., *The Scenery and Antiquities of Ireland* (London, 1842)

Battersby, W., *A history of all the abbeys, convents, churches, and other religious houses of the order particularly of the Hermits of St. Augustine in Ireland* (Dublin, 1856)

Borlase, W., *The Dolmens of Ireland* (London, 1897)

Brash, R., *The Ecclesiastical Architecture of Ireland* (London, 1875)

Brewer, J. N., *The beauties of Ireland: being original delineations, topographical, historical, and biographical of each county* (London, 1823)

Burke, Sir Bernard, *A Genealogical and Heraldic Dictionary of the Landed Gentry of Great Britain and Ireland* (London, 1871)

— *A Genealogical and Heraldic Dictionary of the Landed Gentry of Ireland* (London, 1912)

Chambers, Sir William, *The Decorative Part of Civil Architecture* (London, 1862)

Champneys, A., *Irish Ecclesiastical Architecture* (Dublin, 1910)

Colby, T., *Ordnance Survey of the County of Londonderry* (Dublin, 1837)

Coleman, A., *The Ancient Dominican Foundations in Ireland* (Dundalk, 1902)

Connellan, O., *The Annals of Ireland* (Dublin, 1846)

Cooney, G., Becker, K., Coles, J., Ryan, M., Sievers, S., *Relics of Old Decency, Archaeological Studies in Later Prehistory* (Dublin, Wordwell, 2009)

Craig, M., *The Architecture of Ireland, from the earliest times to 1880* (London, Batsford, 1989)

Cunliffe, B., Bartlett, R., Morrill, J., Briggs, A., Bourke, J., *The Penguin Illustrated History of Britain and Ireland* (London, Penguin, 2004)

de Valera, R., O'Nuallain, S., *Survey of the Megalithic Tombs of Ireland, County Clare* (Dublin, The Stationary Office, 1961)

Doyle, J.B, *Tours in Ulster* (Dublin, 1854)

Duffy, J., *Mellifont Abbey* (Roscrea, 1897)

Edwards, N., *The Archaeology of Early Medieval Ireland* (London, Batsford, 1990)

Fraser, J., *A Handbook for Travellers in Ireland* (Dublin, 1844)

Getty, E., *Notices of the Round Towers of Ulster* (Dublin, 1853)

Grose, F., *The Antiquities of Ireland* (London, 1791)

Harbison, P., *Guide to the National and Historic Monuments of Ireland* (Dublin, Gill & Macmillan, 1992)

Hardy, D., *The Holy Wells of Ireland* (Dublin, 1840)

Harvey, N., *Parochial History of Waterford and Lismore* (Waterford, 1912)

Haverty, M., *The History of Ireland* (Dublin, 1867)

Hogan, A., *Kilmallock Dominican Priory, an architectural perspective, 1291–1991* (Kilmallock, 1991)

Hull, E., *Early Christian Ireland* (Dublin, 1905)

Jones, C., *Temples of Stone* (Cork, The Collins Press, 2007)

Joyce, P. W., *The Origin and History of Irish Place Names* (Dublin, 1913)

Keane, M., *The Towers and Temples of Ancient Ireland* (Dublin, 1867)

Knox, H., *A History of the County of Mayo* (Dublin, 1908)

Leask, H. G., *Irish Castles and Castellated Houses* (Dundalk, Dundalgan Press, 1941)

— *Irish Churches and Monastic Buildings Vol. 1,2,3* (Dundalk, Dundalgan Press, 1955–1960)

Ledwich, E., *Antiquities of Ireland* (Dublin, 1804)

Leet, A., *A Directory to the Market Towns, Villages, Gentlemen's Seats, and Other Noted Places in Ireland* (Dublin, 1814)

Lewis, S. I, *A Topographical Dictionary of Ireland* (London, 1837)

Lynch, A., *Tintern Abbey, Co. Wexford: Cistercians and Colcloughs; excavations 1982–2007* (Dublin, Department of the Arts, Heritage and the Gaeltacht, 2010)

Mac Neill, M., *Máire Rua, Lady of Leamaneh.* (Whitegate, Ballinakella Press, 1990)

Martin, F. X. *The Augustinian Friaries in pre-Reformation Ireland* (Louvain, 1956)

Meehan, Rev. C. P., *The Rise and Fall of The Irish Franciscan Monasteries* (Dublin, 1870)

Moody, T. W., Martin, F. X., *The Course of Irish History* (Cork, Mercier Press, 2001)

Ní Mhaonaigh, M., *Brian Boru: Ireland's Greatest King?* (Dublin, The History Press, 2006)

O'Curry, E., *On the Manners and Customs of the Ancient Irish* (Dublin, 1873)

O'Dalaigh, B., *The Strangers Gaze: Travels in County Clare: 1534–1950* (Ennis, CLASP Press, 1998

O'Donovan, J., Curry, E., *The Antiquities of County Clare: Ordnance Survey Letters 1839,* (Ennis, CLASP Press, 1997)

O'Hanlon, Rev. John, *Lives of the Irish Saints* (Dublin, 1875)

O'Keeffe, T., *Medieval Ireland, an Archaeology* (Stroud, Tempus, 2000)

Petrie, G., *The Ecclesiastical Architecture of Ireland* (Dublin, 1845)

Power, Rev. Patrick, *The Place Names of Decies* (London, 1907)

Russell, T., *Beauties and Antiquities of Ireland* (London, 1897)

Ryan, J., *The History and Antiquities of Carlow* (Dublin, 1833)

Ryland, Rev. Richard, *The History, Topography and Antiquities of the County and City of Waterford* (London, 1894)

Rynne, C., *Industrial Ireland, 1750–1930, an Archaeology* (Cork, The Collins Press, 2006)

Seward, W., *Topographia Hibernica* (Dublin, 1795)

Stalley, R., *The Cistercian Monasteries of Ireland* (Newhaven & London, Yale University Press, 1987)

Stevenson, J., *A Frenchman's Walk through Ireland* (Dublin, 1917)

Stokes, W., *The Birth and Life of St Moling* (London, 1907)

Sweetman, D., *The Medieval Castles of Ireland* (Cork, The Collins Press, 2005)

Trimble, W., *Trimble's History of Enniskillen* (Enniskillen, 1919)

Waddell, J., *The Prehistoric Archaeology of Ireland* (Dublin, Wordwell, 2010)

Wakeman, W., *Wakeman's Handbook of Irish Antiquities* (Dublin, 1903)

Wallace, P. F., Ó Floinn, R., *Treasures of the National Museum of Ireland, Irish Antiquities* (Dublin, Gill & Macmillan, 2002)

Walcott, M., *The Minister and Abbey Ruins of the United Kingdom* (London, 1860)

Ware, Sir James, *The Antiquities and History of Ireland* (Dublin, 1705)

Westropp, T., *The Antiquities of Limerick and its Neighbourhood* (Dublin, 1916)

Wiggins, K., *Anatomy of a Siege, King John's Castle Limerick, 1642* (Bray, 2000)

JOURNALS

Abbreviations

AH	*Archivium Hibernicum*
AI	*Archaeology Ireland*
CLAHJ	*Journal of the County Louth Archaeological and Historical Society*
CR	*Clogher Record*
DHR	*Dublin Historical Record*
HI	*History Ireland*
IAR	*Irish Arts Review*
IUR	*Irish University Review*
JCAHS	*Journal of the Cork Archaeological and Historical Society*
JGAHS	*Journal of the Galway Archaeological and Historical Society*
JIA	*The Journal of Irish Archaeology*
JKSEIAS	*The Journal of the Kilkenny and South-East of Ireland Archaeological Society*
JLFC	*Journal of the Limerick Field Club*
JRHAAI	*The Journal of the Royal Historical and Archaeological Association of Ireland*
JRSAI	*The Journal of the Royal Society of Antiquaries of Ireland*
KAM	*Kerry Archaeological Magazine*
NMAJ	*North Munster Antiquarian Journal*
PRIA	*Proceedings of the Royal Irish Academy*
SAJADHS	*Seanchas Ardmhacha: Journal of the Armagh Diocesan Historical Society*
TDPJ	*The Dublin Penny Journal*
TIM	*The Irish Monthly*
TINJ	*The Irish Naturalists' Journal*
TIPJ	*The Irish Penny Journal*
TLHR	*The Linen Hall Review*
TOC	*The Other Clare*
TPTOUCHS	*The Past: The Organ of the Uí Cinsealaigh Historical Society*
TRIA	*The Transactions of the Royal Irish Academy*
UJA	*Ulster Journal of Archaeology*

ANTRIM

Antrim Round Tower

S. M. S., 'Antrim Round Tower', *TDPJ*, Vol. 2, No. 55 (20 Jul 1833)

Ballymacaldrack Court Tomb

Collins, A. E. P., 'Dooey's Cairn, Ballymacaldrack, County Antrim', *UJA*, Third Series, Vol. 39 (1976)

Bonamargy Friary

Bell, J. L., McNeill, T., 'Bonamargy Friary, County Antrim', *UJA*, Third Series, Vol. 61 (2002)

Craigs Passage Tomb

Williams, B. B., 'A Passage Tomb at Craigs, County Antrim', *UJA*, Third Series, Vol. 50 (1987)

Dunluce Castle

D. A. C, 'Dunluce Castle, Co. Antrim', *TINJ*, Vol. 4, No. 3 (May 1932)

ARMAGH

Ballykeel Portal Tomb

Collins, A. E. P., 'Ballykeel Dolmen and Cairn, Co. Armagh', *UJA*, Third Series, Vol. 28 (1965)

Ballymacdermot Court Tomb

Collins, A. E. P., Wilson, B. C. S., Gay, F. W., 'The Excavation of a Court Cairn at Ballymacdermot, Co. Armagh', *UJA*, Third Series, Vol. 27 (1964)

Killevy Churches

Davies, O., 'Killeavy Churches', *CLAHJ*, Vol. 9, No. 2 (1938)

Murray, D. P., 'A Forgotten Saint', *CLAHJ*, Vol. 5, No. 3 (Dec 1923)

Kilnasaggart Pillar Stone

Morris, H., 'Kilnasaggart Stone', *CLAHJ*, Vol. 1, No. 1 (Jul 1904)

Quinn, J., Ua Cuinn, S., 'Kilnasagart', *CLAHJ*, Vol. 2, No. 2 (Sep 1909)

Reade, G. H., 'The Pillar-Stone of Kilnasaggart', *JKSEIAS*, New Series, Vol. 1, No. 2 (1857)

Reeves, W., 'Kilnasaggart', *UJA*, First Series, Vol. 1 (1853)

Navan Fort

Hamlin, A., 'Emain Macha: Navan Fort', *SAJADHS*, Vol. 11, No. 2 (1985)

Lynn, C., 'Navan Fort—Legendary Capital of Prehistoric Ulster', *AI*, Heritage Guide No. 40 (Jun 2008)

Mallory, J. P., 'Navan Fort', *TLHR*, Vol. 2, No. 1 (spring 1985)

CARLOW

Ballyloughan Castle

de Paor, L., 'Excavations at Ballyloughan Castle, Co. Carlow', *JRSAI*, Vol. 92, No. 1 (1962)

Anon., 'Ballyloughan Castle', *TDPJ*, Vol. 3, No. 136 (7 Feb 1835)

Carlow Castle

Anon., 'The Origins of Carlow Castle', *AI*, Vol. 11, No. 3 (autumn 1997)

H., 'Carlow Castle', *TDPJ*, Vol. 3, No. 108 (26 Jul 1834)

St Mullin's Monastic Settlement

Ffrench, J. F. M., 'St. Mullins, Co. Carlow', *JRSAI*, Fifth Series, Vol. 2, No. 4 (Dec 1892)

Manning, C., 'An Early Catholic Church at St. Mullin's, Co. Carlow', *JRSAI*, Vol. 129 (1999)

CAVAN

Clogh Oughter Castle

Kirker, S. K., 'Cloughoughter Castle, County Cavan', *JRSAI*, Fifth Series, Vol. 1, No. 4 (4th quarter, 1890)

Cohaw Court Tomb

Keenan, E., Kilbride-Jones, H. E., 'Double Horned Cairn at Cohaw, County Cavan', *PRIA*. Vol. 54C (1951/1952)

Drumlane Church and Round Tower

Davies, O., 'The Churches of County Cavan', *JRSAI*, Vol. 78, No. 2 (Dec 1948)

CLARE

Brian Boru's Fort

O'Kelly, M. J., 'Beal Boru, Co. Clare', *JCHAS*, part 1, vol. 57, 1-15 (1962)

Corcomroe Abbey

Anon., 'Corcomroe', *JRSAI* , 5 (3) (1895)

Stalley, R., 'Corcomroe Abbey, Some Observations on Its Architectural History', *JRSAI*, Vol. 105 (1975)

B., 'Abbey of Corcomroe, County of Clare', *TDPJ*, Vol. 2, No. 95 (26 Apr 1834)

Westropp, T. J., 'Corcomroe Abbey', *JRSAI*, 10 (3) (1900)

Dysert O'Dea

de Paor, L., 'The limestone crosses of Clare and Aran', *Journal of the Galway Archaeological & Historical Society*, 26 (1955–6)

MacNamara, G. U., 'The Cross of Dysert O'Dea', *JRSAI*, Fifth Series, Vol. 10, No.4 (31 Dec 1900)

MacNamara, G. U., 'The Ancient Stone Crosses of Ui-Fearmaic, County Clare: Part I', *JRSAI*, Fifth Series, Vol. 9, No. 3 (30 Sep 1899)

O'Farrell, F., 'Dysert O'Dea: The Monks of Dysert O'Dea', *AI*, Vol. 18, No. 3 (autumn 2004)

Westropp, T. J., 'Churches with Round Towers in Northern Clare. (Part II)', *JRSAI*, Fifth Series, Vol. 4, No. 2 (Jun 1894)

Poulnabrone Portal Tomb

Lynch, A., 'Poulnabrone: A Stone in Time', *AI*, Vol. 2, No. 3 (Autumn 1988)

Lynch, A., Ó Donnabhain, 'Poulnabrone Portal Tomb', *TOC* 18, 5-7 (1994)

Quin Friary

Martin, R., 'The Franciscan houses of Thomond in 1616', *NMAJ*, 10/2 (1967)

Westropp, T. J., 'The Last Friars of Quin, Co. Clare', *JRSAI*, Fifth Series, Vol. 4, No. 1 (Mar 1894)

Westropp, T. J., 'Notes on the Franciscan Abbey, Manister Cuinche, or Quin, Co. Clare', *JRHAAI*, Fourth Series, Vol. 8, No. 73/74 (Jan–Apr 1888)

CORK

Kanturk Castle

Anon., 'Kanturk Castle', *TDPJ*, Vol. 3, No. 108 (26 Jul 1834)

McCarthy, S. T., 'The Clann Carthaigh', *KAM*, Vol. 2, No. 12 (Mar 1914)

DERRY

Ballybriest Court Tomb

Evans, E. E., 'Excavations at Carnanbane, County Londonderry: A Double Horned Cairn', *PRIA*. Vol. 45C (1939/1940)

Hurl, D. P., Murphy, E. M., 'The Excavation of a Wedge Tomb at Ballybriest, County Londonderry', *UJA*, Third Series, Vol. 60 (2001)

Banagher Church

P., 'The Old Church of Banagher: County of Londonderry', *TDPJ*, Vol. 1, No. 48 (25 May 1833)

Hamlin, A., Waterman, D. M., 'Banagher Church, County Derry', *UJA*, Third Series, Vol. 39 (1976)

Dungiven Priory

Davies, O., 'Dungiven Priory', *UJA*, Third Series, Vol. 2 (1939)

P., 'Abbey of Dungiven', *TDPJ*, Vol. 1, No. 51 (15 Jun 1833)

Tirkane Sweat House

May, A. McL., 'Sweat Houses (Toigthe Alluis) of County Londonderry', *UJA*, Third Series, Vol. 1 (1938)

Weir, A., 'Sweathouses and Simple Stone Structures in County Louth and Elsewhere in Ireland', *CLAHJ*, Vol. 19, No. 3 (1979)

DONEGAL

Donegal Castle

McNeill, T. E., Wilkin, M. A., 'Donegal Castle', *UJA*, Third Series, Vol. 58 (1999)

Grianán of Aileach Cashel and Hillfort

Lacey, B., 'The Grianán of Aileach: A Note on Its Identification', *JRSAI*, Vol. 131 (2001)

McMahon, P., Moore, D., Moore, F., 'Heritage Guide No. 48: The Grianán of Aileach, Co. Donegal', *AI*, Heritage Guide No. 48 (March 2010)

DOWN

Ballynahatty Giant's Ring

Collins, A. E. P., 'Excavations at the Giant's Ring, Ballynahatty', *UJA*, Third Series, Vol. 20 (1957)

Hartwell, B., 'Ballynahatty: A Prehistoric Ceremonial Centre', *AI*, Vol. 5, No. 4 (winter 1991)

Grey Abbey

Brennan, J. V., 'Grey Abbey', *TIM*, Vol. 51, No. 604 (Oct 1923)

Inch Abbey

P., 'The Abbey of Inch: County of Down', *TDPJ*, Vol. 1, No. 50 (8 Jun 1833)

Struell Wells

Cordner, W. S., 'The Cult of the Holy Well', *UJA*, Third Series, Vol. 9 (1946)

DUBLIN

Ballyedmonduff Wedge Tomb

Ó Ríordáin, S. P., de Valéra, R., 'Excavation of a Megalithic Tomb at Ballyedmonduff, Co. Dublin', *PRIA*. Vol. 55C (1952/1953)

Casino at Marino

Johnson, D. J., 'The Casino at Marino', *IAR* (1984–1987), Vol. 1, No. 3 (autumn 1984)

Kilmainham Gaol

Nowlan, A. J., 'Kilmainham Jail', *DHR*, Vol. 15, No. 4 (Jan 1960)

Martin, L. C., Tighe, J., 'Kilmainham Jail', *DHR*, Vol. 18, No. 4 (Sep 1963)

O'Dwyer, R., 'THE WILDERNESS YEARS: KILMAINHAM GAOL, 1924-1960', *HI*, Vol. 18, No. 6 (November/December 2010)

Rathfarnham Castle

MacMahon, T., 'Rathfarnham Castle', *DHR*, Vol. 41, No. 1 (Dec 1987)

Madden, G., 'Rathfarnham Castle', *IAR* (1984-1987), Vol. 4, No. 1 (spring 1987)

Scantlebury, C., 'Rathfarnham Castle', *DHR*, Vol. 12, No. 1 (Feb 1951)
Tibradden Cairn
Farrington, A., 'The Prehistoric Burial Cairn on Tibradden Mountain, Co. Dublin', *JRSAI*, Seventh Series, Vol. 3, No. 2 (31 Dec 1933)

FERMANAGH
Devenish Island Monastic Site
Ralegh Radford, C. A., 'Devenish', *UJA*, Third Series, Vol. 33 (1970)
Wakeman, W. F., 'The Antiquities of Devenish', *JRHAAI*, Fourth Series, Vol. 3, No. 17 (Jan 1874)
Monea Castle
Earl of Belmore, 'Monea Castle and the Hamiltons', *UJA*, Second Series, Vol. 2, No. 2 (Jan 1896)
Tully Castle
Ó Néill, J. J., Williams, B., 'Near Unto the Bawne: Identifying Sir John Hume's Village at Tully Castle, County Fermanagh', *UJA*, Third Series, Vol. 61 (2002)
Waterman, D. M., 'Tully Castle, Co. Fermanagh', *UJA*, Third Series, Vol. 22 (1959)

GALWAY
Derryhivenny Castle
Leask, H. G., 'Derryhivenny Castle, Co. Galway', *JGAHS*, Vol. 18, No. 1/2 (1938)
Portumna Castle
Fenlon, J., 'Portumna Restored', *IAR* (2002), Vol. 20, No. 3 (autumn 2003)
Knox, H. T., 'Portumna and the Burkes', *JGAHS*, Vol. 6, No. 2 (1909)
Ross Errilly Friary
Mooney, C., 'The Friary of Ross: Foundation and Early Years', *JGAHS*, Vol. 29, No. 1/2 (1960)

KERRY
Cahergal Cashel
Lecky, J., M. J. D., 'Notes on Some Kerry Antiquities: Cahergal and Other Forts', *KAM*, Vol. 3, No. 13 (Oct 1914)
Gallarus Oratory
Henry, F., 'Early Irish Monasteries, Boat-Shaped Oratories and Beehive Huts', *CLAHJ*, Vol. 11, No. 4 (1948)
Olden, T., 'The Oratory of Gallerus', *PRIA* (1889-1901), Vol. 3 (1893–1896)
Kilmalkedar Church
Hill, A., 'Kilmalkedar', *JRHAAI*, Third Series, Vol. 1, No. 2 (1869)
Westropp, T. J., 'Kilmalkedar', *JRSAI*, Fifth Series, Vol. 1, No. 8 (4th quarter, 1891)
Muckross Friary
Graves, J., 'Note of Excursions to Muckross Abbey and Inisfallen; Ardfert and Barrow-nEanach; Aghadoe and Dunloe', *JRHAAI*, Fourth Series, Vol. 6, No. 58 (Apr 1884)
Romilly Allen, J., 'Notes on the Antiquities in Co. Kerry Visited by the Royal Society of Antiquaries of Ireland and the Cambrian Archaeological Association, August, 1891', *JRSAI*, Fifth Series, Vol. 2, No. 3 (Oct 1892)
Ross Castle
P., 'Ross Castle, Killarney', *TIPJ*, Vol. 1, No. 37 (13 Mar 1841)
Anon., 'The Surrender of Ross Castle, Killarney, 22nd June, 1652', *KAM*, Vol. 4, No. 19 (Oct 1917)
Skellig Michael Monastery
de Paor, L., 'A Survey of Sceilg Mhichíl', *JRSAI*, Vol. 85, No. 2 (1955)
S. M., 'The Skelligs', *KAM*, Vol. 2, No. 11 (Oct 1913)

KILDARE
Jigginstown House
Craig, M., 'New Light on Jigginstown', *UJA*, Third Series, Vol. 33 (1970)
Kilteel Castle
Anon., 'Kilteel Castle, County of Kildare', *TDPJ*, Vol. 2, No. 68 (19 Oct 1833)
Moone High Cross
Stokes, M., Westropp, T. J., 'Notes on the High Crosses of Moone, Drumcliff, Termonfechin, and Killamery', *TRIA*, Vol. 31 (1896/1901)
Punchestown Standing Stone
Leask, H. G., 'The Long Stone, Punchestown, Co. Kildare', *JRSAI*, Seventh Series, Vol. 7, No. 2 (31 Dec 1937)

KILKENNY
Dunmore Cave
Coleman, J. C., Dunnington, N.J., 'Dunmore Cave, Co. Kilkenny', *PRIA*. Vol. 53B (1950/1951)

Drew, D. P., Huddart, D., 'Dunmore Cave, County Kilkenny: A Reassessment', *PRIA*. Vol. 80B (1980)

Jerpoint Abbey

Langrishe, R., 'Notes on Jerpoint Abbey, County Kilkenny', *JRSAI*, Fifth Series, Vol. 36, No. 2 (30 Jun 1906)

Rae, E. C., 'The Sculpture of the Cloister of Jerpoint Abbey', *JRSAI*, Vol. 96, No. 1 (1966)

Killamery High Cross

Stokes, M., Westropp, T. J., 'Notes on the High Crosses of Moone, Drumcliff, Termonfechin, and Killamery', *TRIA*, Vol. 31 (1896/1901)

Knockroe Passage Tomb

O'Sullivan, M., 'A Platform to the past: Knockroe Passage Tomb', *AI*, Vol. 10, No. 2 (summer 1996)

O'Sullivan, M., 'Recent Investigations at Knockroe Passage Tomb', *JRSAI*, Vol. 123 (1993)

O'Sullivan, M., 'The Art of the Passage Tomb at Knockroe, County Kilkenny', *JRSAI*, Vol. 117 (1987)

LAOIS

Dunamase Castle

Anon., 'The Rock of Dunamase', *AI*, Vol. 9, No. 2 (summer 1995)

O'Conor, K., 'Dunamase Castle', *JIA*, Vol. 7 (1996)

Killeshin Church

Crawford, H. S., 'Carvings from the Doorway of Killeshin Church, near Carlow', *JRSAI*, Sixth Series, Vol. 8, No. 2 (31 Dec 1918)

Crawford, H. S., Leask, H. G., 'Killeshin Church and Its Romanesque Ornament', *JRSAI*, Sixth Series, Vol. 15, No. 2 (31 Dec 1925)

Timahoe Round Tower

Crawford, H. S., 'The Round Tower and Castle of Timahoe', *JRSAI*, Sixth Series, Vol. 14, No.1 (30 Jun 1924)

LEITRIM

Corracloona Court Tomb

Kilbride-Jones, H. E., 'The Excavation of a Cairn with Kennel-Hole Entrance at Corracloona, Co. Leitrim', *PRIA*. Vol. 74C (1974),

Lowry-Corry, D., 'Cairn at Corracloona, Co. Leitrim', *JRSAI*, Seventh Series, Vol. 7, No. 2 (31 Dec 1937)

Creevelea Friary

Crawford, H. S., 'Carvings in the Cloisters at Creevelea Abbey, County Leitrim', *JRSAI*, Sixth Series, Vol. 6, No. 2 (31 Dec 1916)

MacKenna, J. E., Scott W. A., 'The Franciscan Friary of Creevelea, in the Barony of Breffny, Co. Leitrim', *UJA*, Second Series, Vol. 5, No. 4 (Sep 1899)

Fenagh Churches

Hynes, J., 'St. Caillin', *JRSAI*, Seventh Series, Vol. 1, No.1 (30 Jun 1931)

Murphy, D., 'On an Ancient Ms. Life of St. Caillin of Fenagh, and on His Shrine', *PRIA* (1889–1901), Vol. 1 (1889–1891)

Murphy, D., 'The Shrine of St. Caillin of Fenagh', *JRSAI*, Fifth Series, Vol. 2, No. 2 (Jul 1892)

LIMERICK

Duntryleague Passage Tomb

Kirwan, S., 'Co. Limerick', *AI*, 5 (1991)

Lynch, P. J., 'Cromleacs in County Limerick, no. 5', *JLFC*, 3 (1908)

Lynch, P. J., 'Topographical Notes on the Barony of Coshlea, Co. Limerick, including Lackelly, the Lake District, Cenn Abrat, Claire, Tara Luachra, &c.', *JRSAI* 10, No. 2 (1920)

Westropp, T. J., 'On Certain Typical Earthworks and Ring-Walls in the County Limerick. Part II. The Royal Forts in Coshlea', *PRIA* 33 (1916/1917)

Grange Stone Circle

Ó Ríordáin, S. P., 'Lough Gur Excavations: The Great Stone Circle (B) in Grange Townland', *PRIA* 54 (1951/1952)

Kilmallock Abbey

Anon., 'Proceedings and Papers', *JRHAAI*, 9, No. 80 (1889)

Crowe, J., 'Notice of the Kilmallock Chalice', *JRHAAI*, 9, No. 80 (1889)

Dowd, J., 'Kilmallock, County Limerick', *JRHAAI*, 9, No. 80 (1889)

King John's Castle

Sweetman, D., 'Archaeological excavations at King John's Castle, Limerick', *PRIA*, 80C (1980)

Westropp, T. J., 'The Ancient Castles of the County of Limerick (North-Eastern Baronies)', *PRIA*, 26 (1906/1907)

Wiggins, K., 'Strange Changes at King John's Castle', *AI*, Vol. 5, No. 3 (1991)

LONGFORD

Inchcleraun Island Monastic Site

Wilson, J. M., 'Lough Ree and the Island of Inchcleraun', *JRSAI*, Fifth Series, Vol. 3, No. 3 (Sep 1893)

LOUTH

Castleroche Castle

H. G. T., 'A Hosting at Castle Roche, 1561', *CLAHJ*, Vol. 3, No. 4 (Nov 1915)

McNeill, C., 'Castletown and Roche', *CLAHJ*, Vol. 6, No. 1 (Dec 1925)

Clochafarmore Standing Stone

Muirgheasa, E. U., 'Cuchulainn's Pillar Stone', *CLAHJ*, Vol. 1, No. 4 (Oct 1907)

Mellifont Abbey

Moss, R., 'Mellifont: From Monastery to Mansion', *IAR* (2002), Vol. 24, No. 3 (autumn 2007)

Leask, H. G., 'Mellifont Abbey', *CLAHJ*, Vol. 11, No. 1 (1945)

Stalley, R. A., 'Mellifont Abbey: A Study of Its Architectural History', *PRIA*. Vol. 80C (1980)

Monasterboice

Garry, J., 'The Monasterboice Inscriptions', *SAJADHS*, Vol. 14, No.1 (1990)

Hunt, J., 'The Cross of Muiredach, Monasterboice', *JRSAI*, Vol. 81, No. 1 (1951)

Proleek Tombs

Cole, G. A. J., 'Proleek Cromleck', *CLAHJ*, Vol. 5, No. 1 (Dec 1921)

Lloyd, J. H., 'The Legend of Proleek', *CLAHJ*, Vol. 1, No. 3 (Sep 1906)

MAYO

Moyne Friary

O'Hara, M., 'Rosserk and Moyne, Co. Mayo', *JRSAI*, Fifth Series, Vol. 8, No. 3 (30 Sep 1898)

Rosserk Friary

O'Hara, M., 'Rosserk and Moyne, Co. Mayo', *JRSAI*, Fifth Series, Vol. 8, No. 3 (30 Sep 1898)

Strade Abbey

Mooney, C., 'The Franciscans in County Mayo', *JGAHS*, Vol. 28 (1958/1959)

MEATH

Bective Abbey

Leask, H. G., 'Bective Abbey, Co. Meath', *JRSAI*, Sixth Series, Vol. 6, No. 1 (30 Jun 1916)

Brú na Bóinne

Candon, A., O'Kelly, C., 'An Early Nineteenth Century Description of Newgrange, County Meath', *JRSAI*, Vol. 114 (1984)

Condit, T., 'The Making of Newgrange', *AI*, Vol. 11, No. 3, Supplement: Brú na Bóinne (autumn 1997)

Cooney, G., 'Knowth: The Sequence of Activity', *AI*, Vol. 11, No. 3, Supplement: Brú na Bóinne (autumn 1997)

Eogan, G., 'Discovering Knowth', *AI*, Vol. 11, No. 3, Supplement: Brú na Bóinne (autumn 1997)

Eogan, G., 'A Decade of Excavations at Knowth, Co. Meath', *IUR*, Vol. 3, No. 1 (spring 1973)

Grogan, E., 'From Houses to Henges: The Prehistoric Sequence at Brú na Bóinne', *AI*, Vol. 11, No. 3, Supplement: Brú na Bóinne (autumn 1997)

Harbison, P., 'In Retrospect: The Royal Irish Academy's only archaeological excavation: Dowth in the Boyne Valley', *PRIA*. Vol. 107C (2007)

O'Kelly, M. J., O'Kelly, C., O'Sullivan, V. R., Frith, R. H., 'The Tumulus of Dowth, County Meath', *PRIA*. Vol. 83C (1983)

Hill of Tara

Bhreathnach, E., Newman, C., 'Tara, Co. Meath: A Guide to the Ceremonial Complex', *AI*, Heritage Guide No. 41: Tara, Co. Meath: A Guide to the Ceremonial Complex (Jun 2008)

Conwell, E. A., 'On the Lia Fail on Tara Hill', *PRIA* (1836–1869), Vol. 9 (1864–1866)

Murphy, D., Westropp, T. J., 'Notes on the Antiquities of Tara (Teamhair na rig)', *JRSAI*, Fifth Series, Vol. 4, No. 3 (Sep 1894)

Petrie, G., 'On the History and Antiquities of Tara Hill', *TRIA*, Vol. 18 (1839)

Swan, D. L., 'The Hill of Tara, County Meath: The Evidence of Aerial Photography', *JRSAI*, Vol. 108 (1978)

Kells Monastic Site

Macalister, R. A. S., 'The Ancient Inscriptions of Kells', *JRSAI*, Seventh Series, Vol. 4, No.1 (30 Jun 1934)

Stalley, R., 'Investigating the Book of Kells', *IAR Yearbook*, Vol. 10 (1994)

Trim Castle

Sheridan, P. J., 'The Castle of Trim', *All Ireland Review*, Vol. 2, No. 30 (28 Sep 1901)

Sweetman, P. D., Mitchell, G. F., Mansfield, R. J., Dolley, M., 'Archaeological Excavations at Trim Castle, Co. Meath, 1971–74', *PRIA*. Vol. 78C (1978)

MONAGHAN

Clones High Cross, and Clones Round Tower and Shrine

Barron, T. J., 'The Clones Stone Shrine', *CR*, Vol. 8, No. 3 (1975)

Harbison, P., 'The Clones Sarcophagus: A Unique Romanesque-Style Monument', *AI*, Vol. 13, No. 3 (autumn 1999)

Wakeman, W. F., 'Monastic Antiquities of Clones', *CR*, Vol. 3, Clogher Record Album: A Diocesan History (1975)

Wakeman, W. F. 'On the Ecclesiastical Antiquities of Cluain-Eois, Now Clones, County of Monaghan', *JRHAAI*, Fourth Series, Vol. 3, No. 21 (Jan 1875)

OFFALY

Clonmacnoise Monastic Complex

Bodkin, T., 'Clonmacnoise', *The Furrow*, Vol. 2, No. 10 (Oct 1951)

Manning, C., 'The Very Earliest Plan of Clonmacnoise', *AI*, Vol. 12, No. 1 (spring 1998)

Macalister, R. A. S., 'Clonmacnoise', *JRSAI*, Fifth Series, Vol. 8, No. 2 (30 Jun 1898)

ROSCOMMON
Roscommon Friary
Crawford, H. S., 'The O'Connor Tomb in Roscommon "Abbey"', *JRSAI*, Sixth Series, Vol. 14, No.1 (Jun 30, 1924)

O'Gorman, T., 'Some Remarks on O'Connor's Tomb at Roscommon', *JKSEIAS*, New Series, Vol. 5, No. 3 (1866)

SLIGO
Carrowkeel Passage Tomb Cemetery
Kytmannow, T., 'New Prehistoric Discoveries in the Kesh Corann/Carrowkeel Complex, Co. Sligo', *AI*, Vol. 19, No. 4 (winter 2005)

Macalister, R. A. S., Armstrong, E. C. R., Praeger, R. Ll., 'Report on the Exploration of Bronze-Age Carns on Carrowkeel Mountain, Co. Sligo', *PRIA*. Vol. 29C (1911/1912)

Creevykeel Court Tomb
O'Neill Hencken, H., 'A Long Cairn at Creevykeel, Co. Sligo', *JRSAI*, Seventh Series, Vol. 9, No. 2 (30 Jun 1939)

Queen Maeve's Tomb
Bergh, S., 'Transforming Knocknarea: The Archaeology of a Mountain', *AI*, Vol. 14, No. 2 (summer 2000)

TIPPERARY
Ahenny High Crosses
Crawford, H. S., 'The Crosses of Kilkieran and Ahenny', *JRSAI*, Fifth Series, Vol. 39, No. 3

Harbison, P., 'A High Cross Base from the Rock of Cashel and a Historical Reconsideration of the 'Ahenny Group' of Crosses', *PRIA*. Vol. 93C, No. 1

Carrick-on-Suir Castle
Crawford, H. S., 'Carrick Castle', *JRSAI*, Fifth Series, Vol. 39, No.3 (30 Sep 1909)

Rock of Cashel
Anon., 'Ruins of the Rock Cashel', *TDPJ*, Vol. 2, No. 66 (5 Oct 1833)

Barrow, L., 'The Rock of Cashel', *DHR*, Vol. 29, No. 4 (Sep 1976)

TYRONE
Beaghmore Stone Circles
Hayes, T. D., 'Using Astronomy in Archaeology with a Look at the Beaghmore Alignments', *UJA*, Third Series, Vol. 58 (1999)

May, A. McL., Mitchell, G. F., 'Neolithic Habitation Site, Stone Circles and Alignments at Beaghmore, Co. Tyrone', *JRSAI*, Vol. 83, No. 2 (1953)

Thom, A. S., 'The Stone Rings of Beaghmore: Geometry and Astronomy', *UJA*, Third Series, Vol. 43 (1980)

Castle Caulfield
Jope, E. M., 'Castlecaulfield, Co. Tyrone', *UJA*, Third Series, Vol. 21 (1958)

P., 'Castle-Caulfield, County of Tyrone', *TIPJ*, Vol. 1, No. 28 (9 Jan 1841)

Roughan Castle
Jope, E. M., 'Scottish Influences in the North of Ireland: Castles with Scottish Features, 1580-1640', *UJA*, Third Series, Vol. 14 (1951)

Tullaghoge Fort
Anon., 'Tullaghog', *UJA*, First Series, Vol. 5 (1857)

Hayes-McCoy, G. A., 'The Making of an O'Neill: A View of the Ceremony at Tullaghoge, Co. Tyrone', *UJA*, Third Series, Vol. 33 (1970)

WATERFORD
Gaulstown Portal Tomb
du Noyer, G. V., 'On Cromleacs near Tramore in the County of Waterford; With Remarks on the Classification of Ancient Irish Earthen and Megalithic Structures', *JKSEIAS*, New Series, Vol. 5, No. 3 (1866)

Reginald's Tower
Canon, P., 'The Town Wall of Waterford', *JRSAI*, Seventh Series, Vol. 13, No. 4 (31 Dec 1943)

P., 'The Quay of Waterford', *TDPJ*, Vol. 1, No. 24 (8 Dec 1832)

The French Church
Gimlette, T., 'The French Settlers in Ireland: No. 7. The Settlement in Waterford', *UJA*, First Series, Vol. 4 (1856)

Grant, A. P., 'The Present Condition of the Gravestones in the French Church of Waterford A.D. 1972', *JRSAI*, Vol. 103 (1973)

WESTMEATH
St Féichín's Church
Stokes, G. T., 'St. Fechin of Fore and His Monastery', *JRSAI*, Fifth Series, Vol. 2, No. 1 (Apr 1892)

Fore Priory

Masterson, R., 'The Alien Priory of Fore, Co. Westmeath, in the Middle Ages', *AH*, Vol. 53 (1999)

Seymour, St. J. D., 'Some Priors of Fore, Co. Westmeath', *JRSAI*, Seventh Series, Vol. 4, No.1 (30 Jun 1934)

G. B., 'Fore Abbey, County Westmeath', *TDPJ*, Vol. 3, No. 152 (30 May 1835)

Taghmon Church

Leask, H. G., 'Taghmon Church, Co. Westmeath', *JRSAI*, Sixth Series, Vol. 18, No. 2 (31 Dec 1928)

Hill of Uisneach, 'centre' of Ireland

Donaghy, C., 'Navel-Gazing at Uisneach, Co. Westmeath', *AI*, Vol. 11, No. 4 (winter 1997)

Schot, R., 'Uisneach Midi a medón Érenn: A Prehistoric 'Cult' Centre and 'Royal Site' in Co. Westmeath', *JIA*, Vol. 15 (2006)

WEXFORD

Dunbrody Abbey

Ffrench, J. F. M., 'Dunbrody and Its History', *JRSAI*, Fifth Series, Vol. 6, No. 4 (Dec 1896)

Ferns Abbey

Ffrench, C., Hore, H. F., 'Ferns, County Wexford', *JRSAI*, Fifth Series, Vol. 40, No. 4 (31 Dec 1910)

Ferns Castle

Sweetman, P. D., Mitchell, G. F., Whelan, B., 'Archaeological Excavations at Ferns Castle, Co. Wexford', *PRIA*. Vol. 79C (1979)

Ffrench, J. F. M., 'Ferns Castle', *JRSAI*, Fifth Series, Vol. 40, No.4 (31 Dec 1910)

Rathmacknee Castle

Leask, H. G., 'Rathmacknee Castle, Co. Wexford', *JRSAI*, Vol. 83, No. 1 (1953)

Martin, F. X., 'The Rosseters of Rathmacknee Castle', *TPTOUCHS*, No. 5 (1949)

Tintern Abbey

Bernard, J. H., 'The Foundation of Tintern Abbey, Co. Wexford', *PRIA,* Volume 33, Section C, Nos. 17, 18 (1917)

WICKLOW

Aghowle Church

Corlett, C., 'Heritage Guide No. 54: Aghowle Church, Co. Wicklow', *AI* (2011)

Glendalough Monastic Site

Barrow, L., 'Glendalough and St. Kevin', *DHR*, Vol. 27, No. 2 (Mar 1974)

Fitz Gerald, W., 'Place-Names at the Seven Churches, Glendalough, County Wicklow', *JRSAI*, Fifth Series, Vol. 36, No. 2 (30 Jun 1906)

Rathgall Hill Fort

Becker, K., 'Heritage Guide No. 51: Rathgall, Co. Wicklow', *AI*, (Dec 2010)

Orpen, G. H., 'Rathgall, County Wicklow: Dún Galion and the "Dunum" of Ptolemy', *PRIA*. Vol. 32C (1914–1916)

WEBSITES

www.archaeology.ie
www.doeni.gov.uk

Published in 2017 by
The Collins Press
West Link Park
Doughcloyne
Wilton
Cork
T12 N5EF
Ireland

First published in hardback in 2013

© Tarquin Blake and Fiona Reilly 2013, 2017

Tarquin Blake and Fiona Reilly have asserted their moral right to be identified as the authors of this work in accordance with the Copyright and Related Rights Act 2000.

A CIP record for this book is available from the British Library.

Paperback ISBN: 9781848893047

Design and typesetting by Anú Design, Tara
Typeset in Minion

Printed in Poland by Białostockie Zakłady Graficzne SA